A MOTHER,

A DAUGHTER,

A WEDDING

S0-AVE-461

A MOTHER,
A DAUGHTER,
A WEDDING

Diaries of Bridal Chaos, Conflict and the Bond that Endures

By

Denise A. Kelly

and

Sheila Kelly Kaplan

© 2003 by Denise A. Kelly and Sheila Kelly Kaplan.
All rights reserved.

No part of this book may be reproduced, stored in a retrieval system, or transmitted by any means, electronic, mechanical, photocopying, recording, or otherwise, without written permission from the author.

ISBN: 1-4107-9552-7 (e-book)
ISBN: 1-4107-9553-5 (Paperback)

Library of Congress Control Number: 2003096226

This book is printed on acid free paper.

Printed in the United States of America
Bloomington, IN

1stBooks - rev. 12/11/03

For our husbands, Bob and Gary,
without whose help, support and
patience,
neither the wedding nor this book
would have been possible.

(and possibly for any future, as-yet-
unthought-of grandchildren,
for they should certainly be aware of these
propitious events!—Mother Of the Bride.)

ACKNOWLEDGMENTS

We owe an immense debt of gratitude to our copy editor, Melissa Sperl, and to all our reviewers, who willingly gave up their time to read our early drafts and give us feedback:

> Christine Smith Banks, Roberta Burbank, Suzanne Kubik, Nancy Nagle, Connie Orosz, Diane Sabadish, Sumi Sexton, and of course, once again, Bob and Gary.

This book was greatly improved by their comments and suggestions.

Table of Contents

FOREWORD

DIARY ENTRIES

ONE LAST WORD

FOREWORD

From the Mother of the Bride to other MOB's:

As a retirement present, my dear daughter, "the Bride," gave me a small book written by a Mother of the Bride, who in her preface introduced herself as a "party consultant." Let me make it clear that I have no professional status as a wedding planner. My degrees in Spanish language and literature in no way prepared me for this life-altering experience. Yes, I enjoy cooking and entertaining, but I have done nothing extraordinary in that line. I write this book simply as an ordinary individual who suddenly found herself as the Mother of the Bride, and wants to share her experiences with others who find themselves in a similar situation. This is real life, so it's not just joy recorded here, but also problems and heartaches.

This is an invitation to you to share in our wedding journey. My hope is that these memories will make you laugh with us at some of our missteps. Although you may find some hints in this account, that is not its primary goal. Rather, it is intended to offer you an escape from the inevitable stress of wedding planning, and show what a crazy but wonderful adventure it can be to undertake a project like this with your daughter.

Although we didn't always see eye-to-eye on the details, if we had not been planning a wedding together, this period of my daughter's life would have been so busy that we would not have been able to communicate so frequently. With the wedding preparations, we emailed and spoke on the phone more often than ever before. Each time the phone rang, my husband would roll his eyes and leave the room, knowing the conversation would go on for hours.

If you have outsourced the planning of your wedding, this book may not top your reading list. Had we opted to hire a wedding planner, we could have avoided a lot of grief and aggravation, but then we would have missed the fun and bonding of having done it ourselves.

Planning this wedding was truly a labor of love. Contrary to what the Bride thought at times, I enjoyed every minute of it. And now we've had the added joy of doing a second project together—this book. May you enjoy our account and have a wonderful wedding!

From the Bride to other brides:

Like most brides, I'm sure, I was consumed by moments of panic, frustration, and near breakdown during the planning of my wedding. Often, I didn't even recognize myself. How could a girl like me— career-oriented and "liberated," raised to be socially-conscious and generally unmaterialistic—be reduced to tears at having to choose between calla lilies and gerbera daisies for her bouquet? What happened to the girl who proclaimed she'd email her invitations, and carry a bunch of twigs down the aisle as long as she could marry the man of her dreams? And, most importantly, would anyone involved in planning my wedding (most notably my mother) still be speaking to me when it was over?

I bonded with friends who were engaged or recently married. I heaved sighs of relief when I heard stories of Bridezillas and knew that at least I wasn't as psycho as they were. But, most often, it was my mother who reassured me that I was normal—even lovable—who reminded me to focus on the big picture (the marriage, not the wedding), and who urged me to unload my feelings and to-do list on her, and who always handled it with a smile.

This was the same woman who endured sleepless nights when I chose block printing instead of script for the wedding invitations: the ultimate faux pas.

Few times in a mother-daughter relationship are as tumultuous as the wedding-planning process. You, like me, will probably be surprised by the many contradictions of your relationship—at times awestruck by the bedrock of support she provides, and simultaneously astounded by how completely different her taste is from yours in, well, just about everything.

This book is a tribute to those contradictions. You may see yourself in some of the situations described. It may prompt you to reflect on your own planning experience, and your relationship with your mother. But, above all, I hope that it provides some welcome humor and diversion from your to-do list and the endless parade of appointments.

Everyone's wedding planning experience is different. But the emotions remain uniquely the same. This book is a reminder that what you're feeling is normal, that you will survive, and so will your relationship with your mother.

An Explanation of Terms:

To make reading easier, we've tried to abbreviate frequently-used expressions wherever possible. Thus, you will encounter the following terms:

- MOB. Mother of the Bride
- FOB. Father of the Bride
- POB. Parents of the Bride
- BOB. Brother of the Bride
- MOG. Mother of the Groom
- FOG. Father of the Groom
- POG. Parents of the Groom
- NYC. New York City, specifically Manhattan
- DC. Washington DC
- CP. Central Pennsylvania, that paradise on earth, which you will come to know well from our entries

Also, as an aid to the reader in distinguishing between the entries of the Bride and the Mother of the Bride, those of the Bride are printed in italics. (But we're betting that you wouldn't have needed that to know who was speaking!)

Additional note from the MOB:

The Father of the Bride, recently promoted to this title after 39 years as my husband, was financially intrinsic to the wedding, and unstinting with his overall support. When pressed, he offered opinions. However, he wisely gave a wide berth to all the emotional, endless and seemingly essential details about which the Bride and I agonized for untold hours each day. (This tactic may have saved our marriage!) Thus, when I say "I" or "my daughter," it is not intended to exclude my husband in any way, but rather to reflect his having opted to leave the planning and decisions to the Bride and me.

DIARY ENTRIES

PRELUDE

April to September Two Years Before the Engagement

Part I. April 15.

It started with a vow. A very solemn one.

When I finally broke up with my boyfriend of exactly 2.6 years (you know, the one who's completely wrong for you but you keep dating out of force of habit) at the "ripe old age" of 29, I had to ask myself some tough questions. Like, how could I have dated—even considered marrying—a guy who was such a mismatch for me? What was I thinking? The thought of almost making one of the biggest mistakes of my life gave me chills.

Yes, some introspection was certainly in order. And shortly thereafter, The Vow was made:

"I'm not dating anyone seriously for at least a year."

It wasn't tough to make. After a long-term relationship, I was ready to have fun. Maybe I'd commit to a couple casual dates, but that was it. I needed to find myself *and they would just have to understand. Fueling the fire was the fact that, in two weeks, I was moving from Washington, DC—my home since college—to Manhattan for a new job. And in Manhattan, according to my in-the-know friends, you just don't find the marrying type of guy. Plus, they earnestly added (as if no explanation was necessary), there are a lot of supermodels in NYC.*

Part II. September 20 approximately midnight. Ohm nightclub. Chelsea, NYC.

Vow working well. Job going great. (Amazing, a dotcom that doesn't appear to be going under in the next week.) Loving the inevitable perks that go along with a dotcom job (before everyone came to their senses)—lots of fun parties with free food and an open bar.

Like the one I went to tonight. The Vault.com was having an event, and it was fabulous. As it was ending and we were heading out, my friend started talking to a guy she knew.

As I tapped my foot impatiently, I noticed a guy who appeared to be waiting for his friend to stop talking to my friend. Strangely enough, he also seemed to be dancing by himself. In addition to appearing somewhat inebriated, he was also clearly quite cute, and gave me a winning smile as he twirled around. I laughed at his pirouette and we started talking. He knows my friend's friend—how nuts can he be?

12:15 a.m. Cibar, Union Square, NYC.

I'm only having one drink with him, I told myself, then I'm going straight home. He works with emerging musicians; the last CD I bought was Neil Diamond's Greatest Hits. We couldn't have less in common.

1:45 a.m. Belmont Lounge, Union Square, NYC.

Another glass of wine wouldn't hurt. Besides, he just finished a triathlon three days ago (which is why he's out celebrating) and I've always wanted to do one. He says he'll help me train. And he's really smart and seems fascinated by me—always a good sign.

2:50 a.m. Saying good bye and making a date for the weekend.

This guy is awesome!

EARLY ENGAGEMENT
May to June

19 Months Later

She's getting engaged!
May 10.

My daughter has attracted what I suppose is the normal amount of eligible young men during her dating life, and one after another, has discovered for some reason or another that the current beau was not "The One." A few months after she moved to NYC, we began to hear more about one certain young man, who later came to our house to brave the assembled multitudes for Christmas dinner, and even ate seconds of my broccoli casserole. (I've since discovered he hates broccoli.) Other holidays and family get-togethers did not dissuade him from his purpose, which we discovered to be a serious one.

Yesterday while I was at work, I received a call from my husband, who retired last year and thus was keeping the home fires burning. He was somewhat perplexed because he had received a call from our daughter's boyfriend, checking to see if we would be home and indicating that he wanted to "stop by and see us." To "stop by" was euphemistic at best, since his home in NYC is at least a three and one half hour drive from ours in CP. We wondered aloud, "What could this be about?" while inwardly we both suspected that this could be "The Question." Sure enough, when I arrived home from work, this fine young man had paid us the honor of making a seven-hour round trip to let us know he was going to propose to our daughter that weekend. He told us that we were the only ones privy to the surprise and even showed me the ring, which was lovely. (Obviously, this is one smart guy! He knew how to win me over by letting me be the first one to see the ring!) We had liked him immensely before; now we were even more impressed with his thoughtfulness and the effort he had made to include us in the big moment.

I would be much happier if I could end this entry at this point. Unfortunately, there is more to confess. Our son, who lives in Denver, called this morning, and I was so excited about the news that I couldn't keep my mouth shut. Since I knew our daughter and her boyfriend were safely away in Florida, I told our son of his sister's coming engagement. Mistake! Huge mistake! Really dumb mistake!

I'm engaged!
May 11, 5:35 p.m.

It was no big deal. My boyfriend Gary had told me to keep the weekend of May 9 open, for a "secret surprise" out of town. At the time, I was consumed with practicing for a beginner bellydancing routine my class was performing at the 7th Avenue Festival at the end of May. I was worried that missing a couple of practices during a weekend away might render my shimmy hopelessly broken.

When he asked me to take two days off of work, though, and accidentally let it slip that there were plane tickets involved, I started to get a little suspicious. "It's no big deal," I kept telling myself, "It's not like you're getting engaged or anything."

Okay. It was kind of a big deal. I had moved in with him two weeks prior, and, to be honest, I was really hoping he would propose. Not because I was dying to get married that second. Very soon after that fateful Vault.com party, I figured we would get married eventually, and I wasn't in any particular rush.

No, he should propose so I could prove to my parents that he really was serious. So I could smugly say, "I told you so," to my dad after the "Big mistake, Sheila. Big mistake" speech he made the night I announced I was moving in with Gary, his roommate and their 60-piece shot glass collection. After all that...well, maybe

13

it would be better if he proposed sooner rather than later.

The trip turned out to be a surprise weekend in Florida. When the big moment finally happened, I found it eerily preordained. Like most women I know, I had dreamed about the big moment endlessly, yet when I felt it might happen—as we were walking down the beach for a picnic at sunset—I started to get anxious: "What if I'm so happy I don't cry? I'm so happy right now, I can't imagine crying. But everyone I know cries when they get engaged—will I be weird if I don't?" No need to worry: When he popped the question, I began to sob. The pictures show a tear-streaked face with Cool Whip in my hair (he had the ring buried in a tub of it we were eating with strawberries).

Oh, what a wonderful life we're going to have together. I can't wait.

I have to talk to my mother. May 11, 5:50 p.m.

After about 15 minutes, I began to get fidgety. What good is being engaged if you can't tell someone? Thank God I charged my cell phone before we left for the beach. First call was to my mom—Gary told me he had driven to my parents' house the day before—and I had to go over every detail with my mother. Unfortunately, there was no answer. No problem, I thought: I'll just call my brother Rob in the meantime and tell him the great news.

Except, strangely enough, my brother already seemed to know the news. How could this have happened? Surely my mother—the model of proper etiquette—wouldn't have spilled a secret of this magnitude? When I finally got in touch with her, she had a handy excuse: "Well, I was just so excited, plus I know you and your brother don't talk so often." Nice try. We actually keep our phone calls a secret because otherwise you'll feel left out and demand to know all the details of who he's dating. (Like a typical guy, he doesn't confide in his mother, which drives her crazy.) Remember that yoga instructor with the 2-year-old son he was dating? No? Exactly.

Oops, she's enraged.
May 12.

Today we were at my sister-in-law's house to celebrate Mother's Day, and our daughter, now the Bride, finally tracked us down there. She mentioned that when she hadn't been able to locate us, she had called her brother, who said "Congratulations!" even before she could share her news. What were the chances of that happening? She never calls her brother!

This was a nightmare! Had I ruined everything? I held my breath until she finally told me that her boyfriend, now the Groom, had popped the question before she called her brother. What a relief! I was off the hook for that, but she made a point of telling me that my big mouth could have spoiled the surprise of a lifetime.

She had every right to be annoyed. She then asked if there was anyone I *hadn't* told. There must have been a few (perhaps passersby in the street?) in whom I had not confided, but certainly everyone at the Mother's Day dinner had been regaled with the wonderful story of our son-in-law-to-be coming to see us.

Moral of the story: Keep your mouth shut. Do not share secrets, no matter how excited you are. And keep your mouth shut! This bears repeating, since it is also good advice and practice for my coming state, that of mother-in-law.

A fall wedding—It's a dream come true! May 13.

After basking in the afterglow of engagement for about 48 hours, I sprang into action. I always wanted to get married in the fall. The brisk cool air, the turning leaves, the frizz-free hair...the thought of it filled me with joy. I realized that there was little chance of making October, but November might be possible. I discussed with Gary the grave importance a fall wedding holds for me and my hairdresser, and he agreed we can try for this fall and, if not, we'll just wait till next fall.

I had no intention of waiting until next fall. Gary and I had already dated for a year and a half, 17 months of which we knew each other was 'the One'. I have a demanding job, I have a history of thriving on challenge, I have...a mother. I mean, how hard can it be to plan a wedding in five and a half months?

They're getting married in Manhattan? May 21.

I always thought our daughter would be married in CP. After all, even if she doesn't feel any attachment to the church in the parish we moved to 10 years ago, she grew up in a church just eight miles from here—she would surely be comfortable there. And if she and the Groom should decide on a secular site for the ceremony, there's the beautiful tennis and country club just 10 miles away where I thought we could have both the ceremony and the reception. I could just see her, her dress sweeping behind her as she floated down the grassy slope to the creek, posing for pictures beneath the weeping willow trees. Since it's also a resort, there are charming country accommodations, so all the New York guests could stay there as well. Perfect!

What? They're getting married in Manhattan? Why would they want to do that? Everything will cost four times as much! Besides, many of our older relatives will probably not attend since they would hesitate to go to the big, evil city. Just think of the costs of hotels in NYC! And they're planning the ceremony for 6:30

p.m.? That seems awfully late for guests who are not planning to stay over. And how can I help with the planning? Well, she'll just have to do most of it by herself.

Since the FOB and I were worried that costs would spiral out of control in NYC, we spent quite a long time discussing our financial concerns and reached the following decision: We would give the Bride a sum of money which would be more than adequate for an extremely elegant wedding in CP and let her decide how to spend it. She and the Groom could choose to: 1) spend less than the allotment and use the rest toward a down payment on a house, 2) work within the allotted amount, or 3) add her/their own money to that amount to be able to afford a more luxurious affair.

The Bride has assured me that she does not want to "go overboard" on expenditures for this wedding. I feel somewhat reassured by this statement.

What's wrong with Manhattan? May 21.

She can't possibly be serious. Get married in Central PA? I ponder my close friends from high school for a second: Surely there must be at least one who got married in CP? Finally I widen the circle and ponder all my friends. Were there any who got married in their hometowns? There was my friend Greta who went home to get married. But wait: She was from Miami.

18

Certainly you can't compare a Miami wedding with Mechanicsburg, PA, where—forget a post-nuptial sushi bar—in some parts (my parts) you can't even get a pizza delivered.

This is a problem. When I lived in DC, I could justify not getting married in PA. I lived in DC for five years and had family down there as well. And I'd done myself the favor of dropping lots of little hints along the way about the great wedding I'd have in a rented embassy. Yes, I was always plotting ahead—just in case, you know.

Since I had moved to NYC just two years earlier, though, on a whim with no "roots" here, this was a different story. My parents spoke of my living in NYC in transient terms—as if I were on a mental sabbatical from which they prayed I'd return. Although they enjoyed visiting, certainly they couldn't conceive of my getting married in a place that held no sentimentality and so few memories for them.

I felt bad. I felt guilty. I knew it would be harder for my relatives to attend. And I knew it would be much more difficult for my mother to plan. Not to mention that my parents were footing the bill for the wedding—and had given us a considerably larger sum than most people I knew. And what had their hard-earned money gotten them? The opportunity to make long-distance phone calls to NYC wedding vendors, and to purchase a hotel suite for three nights...

Nonetheless, I ultimately decided that although NYC felt alien to my parents, it held a very special place in my heart as the city where I met and fell in love with Gary. Nearly all of the dating memories we share are from NYC—a place that, believe it or not, is really romantic when you're a couple. The few weekends Gary and I had spent together in CP didn't provide the same attachment for me, even though I have wonderful memories of growing up there.

Thankfully, I have the most wonderful parents in the world and they supported us, as always, in our decision to have the wedding in Manhattan.

Can it be done in just five months? May 23.

As of today, the Bride has informed me that they have a date, a site for the ceremony and reception, and a caterer, all penciled in. I understand now that "not going overboard" means different things to different people, namely to the Bride and me. When she told me how much the building (yes, just the building) would cost, I almost choked. She followed it up with a little financial information on the caterer, and I called for smelling salts. Is it really necessary to have 17 canapés and appetizers? Oh, and let's not forget the sushi station.

What about a band? We went to a party at our country club last weekend. They had a terrific band that has

20

played at club functions before—they're very versatile and easy to dance to. I asked them if they ever played in NYC, and the bandleader said yes, gave me a card and mentioned a price. When I suggested it to the Bride, she didn't sound overly enthusiastic but said she would like to hear a demo tape of them. I've never heard of that—do they do that in CP? I'm learning new things every day. Anyway, it turns out the Groom has already made contact with a band with a singer and five musicians, but since they're on a tour outside of the country, he doesn't yet have an answer. It appears that there are also plans for a string quartet for the ceremony and a musician for the cocktail hour. NYC probably wasn't ready for a CP band anyway! So some of the essentials are falling into place, well, not falling into place—the Bride and Groom have obviously put in a lot of work on this to make these arrangements so quickly. But there's so much left to do.

Emergency...emergency.
May 24.

There are few times you are truly grateful that your fiancée is in artist management. Early on in our relationship, Gary told me to leave the wedding music to him—he has plenty of contacts in the business whom he'd love to book. Unfortunately, he's not as lightning-quick as I am with this wedding planning business, because it's still not done, and we've been engaged for almost four weeks! Doesn't he realize what a life-and-death decision this is?

21

Enter my mother—the Great Problem Solver. Apparently I whined a little too long last week about the lack of musical talent for our wedding. Last night she informed me she'd taken matters into her own hands and has the Country Club band lined up...The Crab Cakes.

Now you are probably wondering, as I was, exactly what kind of a band calls itself The Crab Cakes with a straight face. Quite frankly, I didn't want to find out— visions of an Enchantment Under the Sea theme with Gary dressed as Flounder filled my head. I had to act...fast.

I called Gary urgently at work and finally got through: "How's the band coming?" I yelled. "Did you book Rozz?" "She's touring in the Middle East," he answered. "I sent her an email last week asking her if she's free. What's the problem?" Pause. "My mother has tentatively booked The Crab Cakes for our wedding and if we don't have a band soon, she might finalize a contract with them."

Twenty-four hours later, Rozz was booked.

The bridal gown (Part I). May 25.

Excitement! Today was our first foray into gown shopping. I was afraid that with the wedding being in New York, I wouldn't be able to be involved, but the Bride called last week and suggested that we meet in

Philadelphia and canvass some bridal shops there. We spent hours traipsing through shops, trying on dozens of gowns and trying not to gasp at the prices.

We had talked about what the Bride might want: I thought ivory would look spectacular with her coloring, she thought she did not want strapless, we were both partial to an A-line skirt and a longish train.

Eight hours later, we no longer knew what we liked, but one salesperson made the comment that the Bride "had found her designer" since everything she liked appeared to be by one designer. Designer? That sounds expensive! Basically, I thought she looked gorgeous in everything.

The bridal gown.
May 25.

Despite conducting an all-juice fast for 36 hours prior, gown shopping is somewhat disturbing. Is that cellulite on the back of my arms? Why don't I have a waist? More importantly, why is a plastic comb with netting on it $2000?

First communication with the MOG.
May 26.

Today I received a call from the MOG, whom I had never met before. She wanted to say how happy she was about the engagement. That was a nice gesture—I wish I had thought about making that call first. I guess she has had lots of experience though, since three of her children have already married. She also asked me to let her know if there's anything they can do to help with the wedding. She sounds quite pleasant, which is a relief after some of the horror stories I've heard about in-laws in general, and those involved in the wedding planning in particular.

The Internet comes through.
May 27.

Okay, so we've got the date, the building and the caterer. But there's something missing: It may seem trivial, but I've always thought that a wedding is more effective if you have someone to perform the ceremony. Since this is an interfaith wedding, it becomes a bit more difficult. Fortunately, the Bride and Groom have discussed this aspect pretty thoroughly, made some concessions, and agreed on having two officiants: a Catholic priest and a Jewish rabbi. Fortunately again, both sets of parents support their children's decisions. On the unfortunate side, despite asking everyone we could think of who might have some suggestions or influence, we had not been able to come up with co-officiants.

Enter the Internet. The Bride told me today that she has made contact with an interfaith clergy site through the Internet, and has found that they have an available priest and rabbi for NYC on our date. She has booked the date, and has a meeting scheduled with the rabbi within the week. What a relief! As we suspected, an interfaith wedding is not an unusual occurrence; these clergy have officiated together previously, even at the building where our ceremony will take place. Although the Bride always envisioned herself being married in a church, she understands the level of discomfort this might cause the family and friends of the Groom, and knows that he is making sacrifices too. I'm proud of them both. This spirit of compromise and willingness to sacrifice on both parts is a good prelude to marriage, where it is so necessary.

Finding an officiant.
June 2.

Funny how your priorities change when you get engaged:

> **More important:** *ensuring ribbon color on flower girl dresses matches potpourri sachets in ladies bathroom*
> **Less important:** *securing priest to perform Holy Sacrament of Marriage*

Just so you can put this in proper context, let me preface this by saying that I am, in fact, a practicing Catholic. And, unlike many people I know who view officiants as "hired guns," I actually placed a high

premium on knowing and having a good relationship with the priest who married me.
Which all flew out the window when we decided to get married in five and a half months.

After much nagging from my mother, Gary and I finally started getting serious about officiants. Much to my dismay, I learned that it's really hard to get a priest to leave his parish—including the one you are a member of and give money to—and come to another location to marry you. After more than a few rejections, I started to get panicky. Maybe we shouldn't have put the deposit on the reception place till we had someone to marry us? We took to sharing our anxiety with friends and strangers alike, and they were brimming with advice. One guy we met in an airport in Portland was an Internet-certified minister, and offered his services—at least we had a fallback plan.

And speaking of the Internet, after a couple weeks of dead ends, Gary emailed me a website he had stumbled on: interfaithclergy.net. For a small fee, you can book either a rabbi or a priest, and if you book both you get 25 percent off! Temporarily forgetting that words like "weird" and "wrong" are typically used to describe something of this nature, I quickly contacted them. Within a week we had a priest and a rabbi in our area to marry us.

Finally I can concentrate on my ribbons!

The bridal party (Part I).
June 3.

*Picking your bridal party is about as easy as finding
your soul mate. If you, like me, waited until the ripe
old age of 30 (or beyond) to get married, no doubt the
closet of your adult life is littered with bridesmaid's
dresses. (Let's not even debate whether they can be
worn again.) Unfortunately, some are invariably from
the weddings of friends you haven't felt so close to
since they dropped out of sight when they moved to
another city or confessed that "innocent fling" with a
co-worker. As we all painfully discover through our
twenties, 3 a.m. bonding over pizza in college does not
necessarily make for lifetime sisterhood. However
clear-cut this may seem, the decision not to include
these wayward friendships in your bridal party can be
a difficult one.*

*In general, I tried to use the following litmus test to
determine the friends I would include in my party:
"Could I envision my children using the word 'aunt' to
describe them?" "Did they know and love Gary?"
And, most importantly: "Did I feel that they would do
everything in their power to support and nurture my
marriage?" Although I didn't have to ask myself these
questions of my closest friends, I did for other friends
whose weddings I had participated in or with whom I
had been close. And the answers were generally clear-
cut. Ultimately, you owe it to yourself to be honest
about friendships you don't see withstanding the test of
time and marriage, and to honor those that do by*

asking these women to participate in your wedding. Choosing your bridal party is one time you should put your feelings above those of others and, most of all, above the advice of well-intentioned wedding "experts" who dictate an even number of attendants on both sides so the pictures look good.

The bridal party (Part II). June 10.

The women who will be called "aunt" by your children one day deserve the most amazing bridesmaid's dresses ever. And they shouldn't have to pay a lot for them, either. Needless to say, they should be able to wear them again, too, to New Year's Eve parties, celebrity balls and black-tie events with Heads of State (not necessarily in that order). No, it's never been done before in the history of matrimony, but I am unique. I alone will accomplish this feat, to the great admiration of all my friends.

After hundreds of hours exhaustively scouring the Internet, department stores, boutiques, and bridal magazines, though, I start to get discouraged. This is harder than I thought. Maybe I'm not so special? Everything less expensive is tacky and screams "bridesmaid"; the cute cocktail dresses I adore are $350 and up.

I hit upon it while shopping with a friend in SoHo. We were chatting with the owner of a boutique, who was *proudly completing her latest designer creation on the sewing machine while we talked. Of course! I'll have the bridesmaid's dresses made! Within the hour, we've picked out a beautiful black silk dupioni fabric, and a modified cocktail pattern with simple lines. And she'll make it to their measurements for only $180. It's perfect. I've done it!*

The bridal party. June 12.

Remember that the Bride said she did not want to "go overboard?" When I had previously asked if she had decided on her attendants, she was kind of vague. Today I learned that there are a maid of honor, seven bridesmaids, and three flower girls! This is not going overboard?

The Bride told me that she's having the dresses made. Uh-oh! Bearing in mind that only one of the 11 female attendants lives in Manhattan, I have serious reservations about how this will work. When I tentatively asked the Bride if this might not create a difficulty, she airily proclaimed that it would be no problem, "All they have to do is email their measurements, and she'll mail the dresses to them."

Hmmm, why am I feeling so uncertain? Because, as much as I love her, my daughter has a history of concocting harebrained, safety-net-less schemes, which can culminate in disaster…and I usually pick up the pieces. I'm a bit concerned that this latest plot may have disaster written all over it.

The bridal gown (Part II).- June 15.

Today, somewhat spur of the moment, I decided to go dress shopping again. By myself. I say spur of the moment, because at 5:45 p.m. it hit me that I really need to get a dress soon. I arrived at the shop—which closed at 6:45—at 6:02 p.m. (I knew this, and figured maybe a little pressure might help me make up my mind.)

"Dress shop" might actually be misleading; the place is more like a warehouse, with hundreds of designer dresses, all of them discounted. It's renowned for great fashion and high quality at decent prices. Even better, you don't need an appointment on weekdays.

Giselle, my assistant for the day, watched hopelessly as I tried on about fifteen of my own selections, all of which looked hideous. At 6:35, she asked if I would try one of her recommendations. I begrudgingly said yes. (After all, how could she possibly know what I want?) She returned with a strapless A-line number with beading around the bodice and hem. We slipped it over my head and...I knew. I just knew, the way they say you do when you find "The Dress." My skin glowed, I looked long and lean, and it actually gave me a waist! Finally, the search is over. All I need to do is lose seven pounds and it'll look perfect. I vowed to start my diet tomorrow.

At 6:43 p.m. I floated out of the shop, rewarded my efforts with a maple scone from Starbucks, and quickly called my mom.

She's found the dress.
June 15.

She's done it! I knew she could. Or rather, I hoped that something would eventually satisfy her. The description sounds wonderful, although I'm surprised she chose white when I thought she was leaning toward ivory. And it has a medium length detachable train—hadn't she decided on a long train with a bustle? And it's strapless—I'm sure she said she didn't want that. No matter. She sounds ecstatic. I can hardly wait to see it.

An unfortunate miscommunication.
June 20.

Uh-oh—a bad start for our relationship with the Bride's future in-laws. The Bride had mentioned certain weekends when the Groom's parents were free so we could arrange to meet. When we collectively decided the meeting would not take place until the FOB and I were visiting NYC for the US Open at the end of August, we no longer felt the need to keep the other weekends open. The FOB, realizing that we needed somewhat of a break from wedding issues, promptly purchased a no-refund vacation package in Cabo San Lucas.

A few hours later the Bride informed us that we were invited to an Engagement Party hosted by the Groom's parents the same weekend as our trip. Upon further inquiry, it appeared that the invitation had been extended at some time in the more distant past, but suffered some "desk lag" before being communicated by the Bride to us. Of course, by that point it was too late for us to cancel our other plans. From now on we'll communicate directly with the POG, rather than passing information through the Bride and Groom.

Finding a caterer.
June 22.

Most of our friends are amazed by the devotion that Gary and I have to, well, food. We love eating, cooking and anything related to food, and actually spent one Friday night eagerly viewing our new Cuisinart's instructional video.

Which is why our number one reception priority was, of course, the food. We furiously scribbled hors d'oeuvres notes on cocktail napkins at friends' weddings, and endlessly dissected the relative tenderness of every entrée consumed. And, of course, we wanted the food at our wedding to be "different," in a very chic and exotic kind of way. This, I'm sure, made us number one on every caterer's hit list. Since every couple getting married is highly annoying, you can imagine how bad it was. We went to appointments armed with Food & Wine recipes for the chef to prepare, demanded extra tastings, and actually devised our own Appetizer Ranking System. We were lucky: We found a great caterer who prepared exquisite food, did everything possible to accommodate our whims, and only charged twice as much per head as a five-course dinner at The Four Seasons.

The menu has been decided?
June 24.

The entrees have been determined: Pepper crusted Salmon filet with a light Pesto Cream Sauce, and Crispy Roast Duckling with a Raspberry Sauce. Whatever happened to having a *normal* meal like beef tenderloin? What are my relatives going to eat? Oh well, with 17 appetizers, I'm sure they'll find something. On second thought, the appetizers are extremely non-traditional, too. We'd better arrange for extra baskets of rolls.

Way over budget.
June 26.

I should have seen it coming. I wasn't a math major, but all those big numbers had to add up eventually.

Today I realized with a shock that the combined cost of the room, caterer, band, photographer, and my dress now accounted for exactly 102% of the money my parents gave us. There's no mistaking that negative sign at the bottom of my Excel spreadsheet. Hmmm, what to do...I rack my brains to remember if there is a florist in the family. Does anyone who owes me a favor do calligraphy?

In a panic, I call my mother. Apparently none of my relatives has any wedding-related talents but, as luck would have it, my Aunt Franny just called and said she has a vintage mink stole she wants to give me. Perhaps I could sell that to help finance the remainder of the expenses?

I retire. July 3.

Today was my last day of work, and not a moment too soon! Also today, the Bride confided that her job has become so demanding that she simply cannot talk on the phone while at work, which is generally between 10 and 12 hours a day. Therefore, I will have to be the point person, the one to deal with all the NYC vendors, to ask them questions and get answers, and to make decisions. Will I be able to speak the same language as NYC vendors?

Together we have compiled a list of vendors, contact people and telephone numbers. (Fortunately, we have a long distance provider with very low rates!) We've agreed on "simple and classic" as our overall approach. The Bride assures me that she trusts me to make the right decisions, and anything I decide will be fine. This also pertains to things I see that I want to buy. Let's hope that "simple and classic" has the same meaning for both of us.

It seems as though I'm going from one full-time job to another. How do I feel about this? Nervous, because I'm not sure I really know exactly what she wants. Excited, because we'll be working together toward one of the most important events in her life. Uncertain, because I've left a job I really enjoyed and a boss who gave me lots of positive feedback. Wait, this is scary— is my daughter my new boss? At any rate, my daughter comes first, and this new "job" sounds like a lot of fun!

She retires. July 4.

One of the many great things about being a bride is that people expect you to be selfish. You don't need to cover it up nearly as much as you otherwise would. Take my mother's retirement, for example. As a present, I gave her a custom-made Retirement Survival Kit. Under ordinary circumstances, I would have expended great energy filling it with accoutrements for her to enjoy her favorite pastimes—tennis and gardening. Like a good daughter, I did buy her some tennis clothes and gardening seeds. To be honest, though, these were just window dressing for the main part of her survival kit—a how-to calligraphy book and her very own pen!

The Internet comes through again. July 5.

The Bride and Groom came home for a twofold purpose this weekend: To celebrate my retirement with a party and to decide on invitations. In preparation for their visit, I spent hours at various local printers' shops looking at invitation styles and papers and brought home a number of books for them to review. I had a pretty good idea of what I thought they would want—I was looking for rectangular, cream colored, folded invitations with a traditional black script. The Bride and Groom looked at my selections, then at each other. They did their best to let me down gently, but there was no mistaking the fact that what they wanted was square, white, unfolded cards with gray block printing. This is exactly what I was afraid of—I really don't know what they want! After spending hours combing the entire inventory of CP invitation books, we were still not able to find anything that met their exacting specifications.

About midnight, a sudden inspiration took hold of the Bride. She began to search the Internet and lo and behold, found an invitation site that looked promising. Never one for patience, the Bride promptly picked up the phone and called the owner (fortunately, he was in an earlier time zone) and within an hour had found a style she liked at a price she liked even better. Yes! The owner promised to dispatch a sample of the paper, print style and napkins we were considering. Now, this is an example of "not going overboard" on prices. Maybe she did mean it!

The Internet comes through again. July 5.

There are certain aspects to this wedding that I don't care so much about. My mother tells me that initially invitations were one of them. She claims *I made offhand comments like, "Oh, no one notices the invitations" and "what a stupid waste of money for something you just throw away." I view my mother's recollection with a great degree of suspicion because, frankly, there is* nothing *more important than the invitations, at least not this weekend. Much agony and deliberation is required for a document that will grace someone's refrigerator for 11 days. Why settle for a three-quarter inch border, when one-half inch is so noticeably better?*

The STD's go out. July 7.

Another task that was squeezed into the weekend was the Save The Date letters, affectionately referred to in our wedding lingo as STD's (the *other* kind). The Bride brought along the copy and some interesting stationery and envelopes in a light green onionskin material; we had them printed at a local copy center and set about preparing them for mailing.

After looking at my handiwork in addressing them yesterday, I went to the library today to take out another book on calligraphy. So far, it doesn't look easy! It will be my constant companion, with me at all appointments so that I can practice in all free moments.

The STD's go out. July 7.

I actually spent more time trying to find the STD's than the wedding invitations. I love vellum, but it's so expensive. I finally stumbled upon some in a hole-in-the-wall stationery store, and the owner gave me 100 matching sheets and envelopes for $60. Yeah!

My mother and I spent a couple of hours inserting the invitations into the vellum overlay and stuffing the envelopes. For some strange reason, she keeps referring to it as "onionskin." How is it that two people who are the closest of friends can speak two totally different languages?

FIRST WORKING WEEKEND IN NYC

July 19 – 21

The bridal salon. July 19.

When the Groom is away, the Bride will not play, but will invite her mother for a working weekend. I arrived in NYC by train on Friday afternoon to impending doom—an "end of the world"-looking black sky and, of course, no taxis. I decided to walk/run the nine blocks with my rolling suitcase to the bridal salon where I had arranged to meet the Bride. I arrived sopping wet. The salespeople took pity on me, equipped me with a roll of paper towels, and showed me to a changing room. I emerged, renewed by my towel-dried hair and a complete change of clothes from my suitcase.

41

And there she was. I was bowled over by my first sight of my lovely daughter in her bridal gown. I was nearly speechless, and for me, that's unusual. A mother may know her daughter is engaged, and be engrossed in preparations for the wedding, but the reality of the coming event does not sink in until she actually sees her in her gown. What a vision! She'll be a beautiful bride!

The bridal salon. July 19.

Am I nuts? What was I thinking? Why on earth would I have chosen this dress? The beading is completely gaudy—not at all how I remembered it—and worse, I've recently learned that sheaths with ruffles are what's in now. I'll be hopelessly out of style in an A-line. I should have gotten the dress that girl is trying on. Why didn't Giselle pick that one out for me? This is what I get for gown power-shopping.

The look on my mother's face confirmed my fears. Instead of jumping up and down and/or bursting into tears of joy, she just said how nice I looked over and over again like a robot. Oh sure, she just got drenched in a downpour, but I know it's really because she secretly hates the dress as much as I do. It's all totally, hopelessly wrong. What should I do? The dress is ordered; I've already put the deposit down. But I need to do something. I need a maple scone!

In search of the MOB dress.
July 20.

The next day brought a visit to the famed Bridal Building in Manhattan with its variety of discount bridal stores. Now this was embarrassing! When you find a dress in a color and style you love, but it is size 8 (which is definitely not my size), what do you do? Especially when three salesladies are around you saying, "But dahling, it would be perfect on you. Try it on, just to get an idea of how it looks. We can always order a larger size."

Well, of course you try it on. What else can you do? But first you back very carefully into a corner (in this case, discount meant no dressing rooms) so no one can see you, and tell the salesladies that your daughter will help you with it. No such luck—they follow you, tugging and pulling the front down, and holding the back together to show how flattering the neckline would look on you.

After five minutes of fawning, I happened to glance over my back and noticed that the corner I had backed into was mirrored! The back slit of the dress was resting snugly above my hips, providing a fine view of my backside and legs for the entire store to see.

Oh sure, they make the sample bridal gowns size 12, but the MOB dresses are all size 8. What's wrong with this picture?

MOB meets MOG, July 20

Next on the agenda was the make-up studio, where I was finally introduced to...the MOG! We had spoken briefly right after the engagement when she had called to express how happy she was, but other than that, we had limited contact, and I had never met her in person.

It was an encounter I had been looking forward to, but was also very anxious about. Why? Well, let's face it. This is not an easy situation—meeting someone who's going to be so important in your daughter's future life. I had a number of private conversations, alternately dredging up concerns and reassuring myself before the meeting:

MOB: "I hope she's nice."

Smarter self: "Well, of course she's going to be nice. Didn't she raise the man that your daughter has chosen as her future husband? How could she be anything but nice?"

MOB: "Well, I hope she's not so wonderful that my daughter starts to feel as comfortable with her as with me!"

Smarter self: "Don't be ridiculous! Nothing can change your relationship with your daughter."

MOB: "But she'll be in NY, so much closer than here. The Bride will probably be running over to her house every weekend, while she'll have to plan months ahead and pay hundreds of dollars on rental cars or train tickets to come to CP. They may *never* visit us again!"

Smarter self: "I'm not continuing this conversation if you insist on talking nonsense."

And then there's the stereotype of the New Yorker. Was the MOG going to be model thin and dressed to kill, putting the poor CP MOB to shame with her elegance? What if we didn't like each other? Images crossed my mind of me in my black pants (the Bride tells me that black is always right in NYC), finding nothing to say, seated across from a bored-looking, perfectly made-up, 90-pound beauty in a designer original leather outfit.

And after all that, the MOG was so normal and nice! Completely human. There we were, both of us, in our black pants and beige tops, dressed like twins, conversing effortlessly while watching the Bride have a make-up trial session. Kudos to the Bride for being so clever and planning the first meeting for mothers only!

Bride watches MOB meet MOG.
June 20

Perched in my make-up chair at Laura Mercier, I eyed my mom and Gary's mother across the room. Gary's

45

mother arrived just after I began my session, so I wasn't able to introduce them properly, or act as dialogue facilitator.

Why is this make-up artist so chatty? Can't she tell I'm trying to eavesdrop on their conversation? I fought the urge to leap out of the chair with only one eye done and check on the progress.

From halfway across the studio, I silently begged for success. I saw their lips moving: good sign. Was that...yes! Smiles and laughter. I knew it. Gary's mom is very nice, and my mother can get along with anybody. I finally started to relax and think about which new lipstick I was going to buy.

We meet with the caterers.
July 20.

Next we went to the caterers, where we asked a mountain of questions, decided on place settings, and looked at fabrics for tablecloths and discussed overlays. Overlays? We have table linens but we need contrasting color overlays too? And of course they're an extra charge. Suddenly this is another thing the Bride considers essential to her happiness. Surprise, surprise, the 15 books and 200 selections available do not meet the Bride's lofty requirements. We leave undecided.

More budget woes. July 21.

If nothing else, remember this rule: Everything you budget for your wedding will cost twice as much as expected. Despite the money we saved on the invitations, our wedding deficit continues to mount. I find it suddenly impossible to prioritize. Of course we have to have the best photographer—we'll be looking at these pictures for the rest of our lives! But the best photographer in the world can't hide frizzy, windblown hair, or a shiny face, so I simply must have top-notch hair and make-up artists. Which I couldn't dream of not having for my bridal party as well. And on it goes...

Which brings me to the flowers. To be honest, before I got engaged, I couldn't tell a dahlia from a dandelion, and have absolutely no recollection of the flowers at any of the fifty or so weddings I have attended.

Which is why, when the seemingly endless Bank of Mom and Dad finally ran dry, and we had to make some tough choices, the flowers ranked closer to the bottom. I just couldn't see spending thousands of dollars for something that would be dead before we left for our honeymoon. More to the point, we only had $1900 left in the wedding budget for flowers, which from a Manhattan florist will get you a couple of nice carnation bouquets—if they even agree to do your wedding at all.

My brilliant mother hit upon it during her visit. She had heard about the floral district in Manhattan— surely there must be wholesale florists there? Sure enough, we called a couple in the phone book, and they both said they did weddings. And off we went.

Flowers are frustrating.
July 21.

The first place we visited personified "flower wholesaler." There was no cute sitting room for my mother and me to retire to and peruse wedding books. No floral assistant brought us coffee and gushed about what a beautiful bride I'd be.

But their work spoke for itself. Photos of events they had done were quite impressive, and they seemed to book a lot of weddings. Unfortunately, the owner was out the day we went, so we met with an assistant named Juan.

Juan was extremely pleasant and appeared quite knowledgeable. He had done many weddings, he said, and would love to do mine as well. More importantly, he seemed to think everything I wanted sounded just great.

Take the colors, for example. I wanted burgundy calla lilies for my bouquet, and some type of burgundy flower in every table and altar arrangement. Tulips, roses, callas—I didn't care, I just wanted burgundy!

48

Lighten up each arrangement with some cream or chartreuse flowers, and I'd be a happy camper.

Juan understood this.

"Borrrgundy" he repeated in his accent, after I'd made my speech.

"Yes, that's right" I replied, holding up a burgundy calla. "But I'd like to mix up the kinds of flowers in the arrangements, so I want to find some other types of burgundy flowers, maybe dahlias?"

"Ah yes, borrrgundy dahlias—very pretty," he replied, pointing to a fuschia-colored bloom.

"Well, no, actually not that pink" I clarified. "Burgundy—like this." I waved the calla again.

"Oh, right. Let me see." Juan disappeared into the back and returned with another attempt. "This would be perfect in the altar arrangement" he said, presenting me with a single rust-colored gladiola.

Patience, Sheila, patience. "I agree about the type of flower," I say carefully. "Unfortunately, that's not exactly the color I was thinking of. I want burgundy— that's rust."

Thankfully, my mother is a retired Spanish teacher. She does a quick intervention in Juan's native tongue, and he finally locates some burgundy roses that are

49

beautiful. He also does a sample arrangement, which looks incredible—exactly what I want. The price is even more incredible. "So what if he doesn't know exactly what burgundy is—it can be a subjective color," I rationalized to myself. "I'll give him a swatch and make sure he matches every flower to it when we do the final order."

With just a hint of misgiving, I tentatively book the date with Juan.

Flowers are frustrating.
July 21.

What a relief that Juan finally seems to know what 'borrrgundy' is. Too bad the Bride and I were not as attuned on the types of flower arrangements as we had thought. Since the Bride and I had discussed flowers many times previously, we had thought we were ready to talk to a florist. But as I listened to the Bride telling Juan what she wanted, I thought she was not explaining it well, so I tried to clarify what she was saying. Suddenly, we looked at each other in amazement as we realized that while we had thought we were on the same page on the flowers, in reality we were volumes apart! Neither of us really understood what the other was saying, but one thing was clear: We did not have the same concept of what the flowers should look like. I think we were both hit with a feeling of total frustration.

Flowers are frustrating.
July 21.

Compounding the floral issue was that, well, I couldn't really decide what I wanted besides burgundy flowers. I knew I didn't want really tall arrangements, but not really small either. I love ivy, but couldn't really decide how to fit it in. And, of course, I didn't want to give anything up. Anything is possible with enough creativity!

Surely my mother knew how to fix this. I explained what I thought I wanted to her and she immediately understood. I knew it!

Strangely, however, she started describing something to Juan that was completely different: a low arrangement with ivy coming out of it around the sides. I have a mental picture of a floral spider. Is that what she's thinking? How is it we could have misunderstood each other so totally?

Thankfully, Juan's sample arrangement looks nothing like what I was thinking, or thought she was thinking, but somehow is exactly what I want. And not a moment too soon.

All weddinged out. July 21.

Regardless of the floral issues, we had an extremely productive and enjoyable weekend. I had arrived armed with pages of questions, but by the time the weekend was over, we were so exhausted, and if truth be told, so tired of wedding issues that we never got to all of them. It was a relief to focus on plates of Cambodian take-out and talk about anything except the wedding! I'm feeling a bit more confident that we're on the right track, but I still can't believe that she wanted ivy hanging out of tall vases—it would have looked so dumb!

THE PREPARATIONS INTENSIFY

July to August

<u>*Reception budget—The saga continues. July 22.*</u>

Still Need:
- *6 large candelabra*
- *Small votives and votive holders for all tables (20 dinner and 6 cocktail tables)*
- *Contrasting organza fabric overlays for all tables*
- *Creative and interesting way to display table cards at entrance to reception*

(okay, maybe "need" is a strong word)

Currently Have:
- *$275*

- *37 more guests on list than originally anticipated*

How could I have missed such crucial details when I did the budget? I'd always wanted lots of candles at my wedding, but it seems the wholesale florist doesn't "do" candles, or any rentals for that matter. And the fabric overlays are truly a must, even though most of my married friends from DC don't seem to have heard of them. Unfortunately, our caterer charges extra per table for them—ouch!

Hmmm, what really creative and selfless person do I know who might be willing to pitch in?

<u>Get out the sewing machine.</u>
<u>July 22.</u>

The bride's puppy-dog eyes were more than I could take. She just looked so crushed when we found out that the overlays were going to increase the catering price by nearly a thousand dollars. I admit it: I had a weak moment.

I seem to have volunteered to make 20 large and 10 small silver-gray organza overlays. By myself. Don't forget somehow locating the 60 yards of extra-wide special-order fabric, either.

Rather than dwell on this unsettling thought, I plunged in. I decided to search for the fabric on the Internet and posted my request for 72"-or-wider silver gray organza on a fabric bulletin board. (Yes, there are such things.)

The next morning I received a call from a very helpful gentleman who put it bluntly: "Honey, what you're looking for doesn't exist." Visits to other fabric sites confirmed my fears. The overlays were looking doomed.

Just as I was about to call it quits, up popped an email from Fabric Finders, telling me they had located an 118" width of what I wanted! We'll have to order a huge amount, but I checked with the bride, and she suggested using the extra material for wrapping bridesmaids' gifts. Can I do this, or am I crazy to try?

I discover arts and crafts stores.
July 23.

Finally! Sounds like the Bride has had a dose of budget reality injected into her plans. The discount florist is a start. Could this also mean that we can consider a few other low-budget items? It's certainly worth a try!

One wonderful thing about retirement is that I now have the time not only to scan the newspapers, but to read them completely, and peruse every single advertising circular enclosed in them. Today's find was a great sale on votive candles and holders at a local arts and crafts store. Since the Bride had

57

mentioned she wanted these on each table, I went out to look at them.

Secure in my newfound knowledge that the Bride trusted me to make decisions, I bought 220 fishbowl shaped votive holders and candles. The quandary was what scent and color to buy. By now, I was aware that I had to suppress my natural urge toward cream since the Bride preferred white, but the white votives were gardenia or jasmine scented, which I thought was a bit strong. Further, since we planned to cover the votive holders with burgundy crepe paper, and the color of the candles would not be obvious, I opted for the vanilla-scented, cream-colored candles.

While I was regaling the Bride with the tale of my bargains, I thought I noticed a slight hesitation in response when I mentioned the fishbowl shape. Wonder if she's having second thoughts about trusting me to make decisions?

The honeymoon (Round I). July 25.

Today Gary told me his best man has made a very generous offer: He has offered us the use of his family's houses in Guyana for our honeymoon. (For those of you who are wondering, Guyana is a small country in South America—next to Venezuela. I had to look it up myself.) In any event, his family owns two properties in Guyana—one on the beach, the other on a river in the rain forest. As Gary explains it, we would be given full-run of the (currently uninhabited) houses for one week each, and provided their servants and bodyguards for our personal use. And wouldn't that be a great honeymoon?

Hold on, back up! Bodyguards? *Why is that necessary?*

Well, as Gary explains it, there is some unrest in Guyana. Apparently it's not safe to go anywhere without bodyguards, but since we'll be on the estates most of the time, it won't really matter. Gary rattles on about swimming pools, private beaches and a backyard that backs up against the rain forest and I'm sold. It sounds heavenly. Plus, I've never had a bodyguard before.

I eagerly headed to the Internet to learn more. Unfortunately, Google rewarded a "Guyana resorts" search with a list of...campsites. Oh, well, we don't need to leave the estates—we'll have everything we need there.

Tonight, I called my parents and told them the news. My dad was very excited. "We were watching the Discovery Channel last night and they were hunting giant anteaters in Guyana!"

Good thing I have that bodyguard.

Technology problems. August 7.

Time out for a few philosophical questions. How did we ever exist without the computer? How did people deal with daily life without a telephone? Will our marriage survive if the FOB insists on being on the phone and Internet when I need access to them?

The mistake was in allowing him to retire before I did and have sole, uninterrupted control of our technology, so he became accustomed to being King of the Computer! Doesn't he realize that things have changed now that I am the MOB?

I must admit that I have insisted on being on both the Internet and telephone about 80 percent of our waking hours, which, with a dial-up modem, is causing some problems. And my suggestion that he use the public library's computer didn't go over too well. The solution? High-speed cable modem access, so we can be on the telephone and the Internet at the same time. And it cannot happen a moment too soon!

Table cards creativity. August 10.

The Bride and I have discussed numerous ways to have a really interesting table card display. Well, to be more exact, the Bride has discussed them and I have tried to be supportive. I mentioned the matter to a really creative friend, whose response was, "What's the matter with just setting them on the table?" My sentiments exactly…before I knew my daughter wanted—no, *needed*—this. Funny how what could appear to be too much trouble means nothing to the MOB who is intent on helping her daughter fulfill her every wedding fantasy!

The Bride's suggestion was that we would somehow have a wall of ivy and attach the table cards to it. It sounds eye-catching, but how to do it? I visited a local florist to learn more about ivy, and bought a plant so I could experiment. Brainstorm! What about a white lattice board to be propped up on a table against a wall with lengths of ivy intertwined through the latticework?

I quickly realized that this task will involve enormous amounts of ivy, which dies quickly, and therefore requires water bottles for each strand. Maybe I could learn to sew overlays with my feet while practicing ivy arranging with my hands? Forget it—Juan's getting a lattice board to decorate.

Special events planning. August 12.

The only thing more stressful than planning the wedding has been arranging the Rehearsal Dinner and morning-after brunch. Gary's parents generously agreed to foot the bill, and said we should just choose a place and let them know the cost. Mindful of the fact that his parents may want to retire someday, I wisely interpreted "a place" to mean "a place charging less per head than our wedding caterer." Which, as we discovered, in Manhattan on a Friday night, is no small feat.

We pounded the pavement night after night trying to find some restaurant—any restaurant—that could accommodate a Rehearsal Dinner for 80 people without requiring the mortgaging of his parents' house.

Rhetorical question: How is it that Manhattan restaurateurs can have more of an attitude than wedding vendors? Rehearsal dinner estimates ranged from the ridiculous ("For the budget-conscious, we recommend our gourmet chicken pot pie for $37") to the insane ($20,000 just to reserve the upstairs "Intimate Dining Room"). Finally, when we had almost lost hope, we found Sal—owner of Bondi Restaurant in Chelsea, who agreed to close his doors for the night, and treat our guests to his gourmet Northern Italian cuisine for a very reasonable cost. Even more astounding, he actually seemed to care that we were getting married and seemed strangely uninterested in ripping us off.

Now we just need to figure out the brunch. How hard can that be?

Obsessing over votives. August 14.

I think I've finally lost it. I couldn't sleep last night because I started to worry whether the votives would last the entire five hours of the reception.

I decided to burn a votive in a holder to see if it was safe and to determine just how long it would burn. I then spent my day constantly checking the candle, fretting over it like my firstborn. Good news! It was still burning after eight hours, and the holder was still intact, so it appears not to be a safety risk. I, on the other hand, may be. To myself.

A little concerned. August 15.

My mother's starting to concern me. Today she casually mentioned she's been practicing her calligraphy in the dentist's waiting room. The day before that she had an all-day séance with a votive. I admit, I would never have thought to make sure the candles would last the whole five hours, but I wonder—is this behavior normal?

The worst part? I have created this stressed-out insomniac.

I'm getting worried that she's so concerned about all the details that she won't enjoy the wedding itself. More than anything, I want her to feel relaxed on the big day so she can appreciate all our hard work. So I told her what I was thinking: that we should hire a wedding coordinator for the day of the wedding. Gary and I are adding our own money to pay for the extra guests and what remains to be purchased, and there's still some left.

In typical fashion, she tells me that's not necessary. She's confident that the caterers and the band will be just fine if she gives them a detailed schedule, and that she doesn't need help managing them.

With some reservations, I let her talk me out of it. I hope she's right.

The craft store declares me persona non grata. August 17.

New decision: no burgundy crepe paper and white ribbon to be wrapped around votive holders. The crepe paper may make it too dark.

New problem: now the cream colored, vanilla-scented votives will be obvious and may not look right with the bright whites we have in the other decorations.

New solution: return 219 votives to the craft store where I bought them. Unfortunately, the same poor woman that had to bring the 220 candles out from the storeroom the first time I bought them was once again on duty when I took them in for exchange. Even more unfortunate, when she brought out the white, jasmine scented votives, we discovered that about half of them were green-tinged rather than pure white. So we had to pick through to find 219 white ones. Only when I was checking out did she tell me that "sometimes the candles change color." Just great! I wondered aloud if it could be due to heat where they were stored; she thought that was a possibility. So now the votives will sit in our basement until October, when I'll check the color again and decide if they need to be returned again. I hope that poor clerk is on vacation if I return.

The MOB dress (a continuing concern). August 18.

A few days ago, I called about the MOB dress I had seen back in July, and who should answer but the owner of the company! I explained that I would be in NYC again at the end of August, and asked whether the dress could be available in my size to try on. He was extremely helpful and said he would try to get a larger sample dress for me. By the time we hung up, we were on a first name basis and I was privy to his doctor's appointments and health problems. I was to call him again before I come to confirm the appointment. I must remember to allow plenty of time for this call.

By now I've visited every department store, bridal shop and specialty shop in our area, with a few side trips to nearby areas, without finding a dress I like nearly as well as the one I saw in NYC in July. The

FOB, who cannot totally ignore my constant agonizing about this issue, came to the rescue by noticing the name of a seamstress in the church bulletin. I called her this afternoon, liked her immediately, and got some references. She can either make a dress for me or alter one, so I can try the NYC dress on with that in mind. One issue partly resolved. I'm sure I'll get a better night's sleep tonight.

The honeymoon (Round II). August 19.

Gary was beside himself with excitement tonight. It appears he was speaking with his Best Man's uncle (who will be one of our hosts in Guyana), and they were planning some Special Honeymoon Excursions for us. The first is a plane trip over Kaieteur Falls, which is the highest waterfall in the world. This I had known about previously, and was really looking forward to. I had seen pictures, and it looked breathtaking.

Tonight Gary informed me there is now a Special Honeymoon Excursion Addendum—after we visit the falls, a friend of the uncle is going to take us sightseeing in the rain forest below. Wow—that sounds cool. Like what kind of sightseeing? Well, some really amazing, unprecedented sightseeing: We'll get to covertly spy on a tribe of cannibals that haven't seen outsiders in over 100 years! The friend goes fishing up there all the time and would love to take us! And wouldn't that be a great Special Honeymoon Excursion?

Before I dashed my future husband's dream of a lifetime, I took stock: This might be the only time I would ever get to see a tribe of cannibals. Could I live with the regret? There was also the chance I was overreacting; after all, we had bodyguards to protect us.

After a careful several-second deliberation, I sweetly informed Gary that I didn't think I'd be accompanying him on the Excursion, but that he was certainly more than free to go without me. Of course, he wouldn't dream of that—he wanted us to experience this perfectly safe sightseeing trip together. I decided to change the subject; there were more urgent decisions to focus on now. And maybe the friend's "risk-taking" lifestyle will catch up to him in the meantime...

67

SECOND WORKING VISIT TO NYC

August 28–30

The MOB dress—at last!
August 28.

FOB accompanied me to the office of my new best friend, the bridal dress company owner, so I could try on the MOB dress again. Yes, he had managed to get it in a larger size. Unfortunately, there was no air conditioning at this discount showroom, and it was an extremely hot day, and stifling in the dressing room. No salesladies either, so my husband helped me into the dress. Yep! The color and style were perfect, and I loved it just as much as I remembered! FOB's challenges were not over, however. When I had the dress halfway off, a hook got caught in the beading, and I suddenly became so hot that I felt suffocated under the lined and beaded bodice. As I gasped for

FOB to "get me out of this," he valiantly tried to extricate me from the dress. I think I heard him muttering something about not knowing this was a part of a daughter's wedding, but I was too relieved to be out of the dress to protest. Despite my two dressing-room disasters, I liked that dress! I decided to order it.

Meeting the groom's parents. August 28.

The day was not yet over. Waiting for us at the apartment when we returned were the parents of the Groom. This was the long-awaited "Meeting of the Parents!" Fortunately, after the MOG and I had met the previous month, we had spoken on the phone a number of times, so that anxiety was long past. The Bride and I quickly freshened up. When we came out to the living room, everyone was chatting comfortably, and the FOB and FOG seemed to be enjoying each other's jokes. Good, another hurdle successfully jumped!

We then headed for Bondi, a nearby Italian restaurant, the site chosen for the Rehearsal Dinner. The POG had managed to snag a parking space right outside the Bride and Groom's apartment building, so they offered us a ride to the restaurant, while the Bride and Groom walked the few blocks there. What a riot! The POG started picking on each other about driving in NYC and how and where to park the car, which set a hilarious tone for the rest of the evening. The food at Bondi was excellent, the ambience charming, and the owner extremely hospitable. He even carried around a basket of fresh figs from his mother's tree, offering them to guests. As so many NYC restaurants, the building itself was long and narrow, which would not lend itself to speeches or a group feeling for the Rehearsal Dinner, but the overall effect was overwhelmingly positive. And most of all, we had a fun evening "meeting the parents."

Morning-after brunch—The quest. August 29.

What a huge relief that the Rehearsal Dinner is planned, and that our parents actually seem psyched about the restaurant! Compared to that odyssey, finding a restaurant for the brunch will be a piece of cake.

Or so I thought. The second I mention the word "wedding," previously reasonable brunch places suddenly require between $40 and $95 per person for a lame buffet of scrambled eggs and assorted muffins! After a few misses, I get smart and begin referring to it as a "large group of friends arriving over the course of two hours." This works fine until I am forced to admit that it will be roughly 100 friends and may require some additional staff.

After scouring at least 50 places, we finally found Pete's Tavern, a cute Irish spot with great food and an upstairs party room we can have for the morning. Like

Sal, they are great to work with and very friendly, which is not something to take for granted in NYC.

There was one other very positive outcome of the brunch quest, though: One of the restaurants we visited was a very chic Asian-influenced place with a number of extremely cool wooden pillar candelabra adorning the entrance and hallways—the precise type of candelabra, in fact, I've been looking for to grace the ceremony and reception but haven't been able to locate. Being the ever-resourceful bride, I told the manager that we'd be happy to pay $50 a head for Asian-influenced omelettes if he'd throw in six of the candelabra. He looked at me like I was out of my mind and Gary hustled me out of there, explaining that I was extremely tired and not thinking straight. Thankfully, the manager took pity on me and followed us into the street, yelling, "I can't give you ours but you should really try Pier One!"

Saga of the candelabra. August 30.

Did I mention that the Bride was determined to have candelabra for the wedding? Although I was not convinced they were necessary, I had researched rent-it centers in CP for availability and cost: We could rent gold-finish seven-taper candelabra for the weekend for a fairly reasonable price, maybe between $250 and $300 for six of them. Knowing that we couldn't possibly lug six candelabra to NYC for the wedding,

along with all the other items we had to take, I was still
sure that we could find something comparable there.

Wrong! First of all, the Bride informed me that she
didn't want gold; she wanted silver. Secondly, she
didn't like the idea of tapers, but wanted pillar candles.
One day she called me saying that she had found
exactly what she wanted at Pier One. They were five-
foot black metal candelabra holding three pillar
candles each. She announced that she was going to buy
them…at $85.00 a piece. I was dumbfounded! To buy
six candelabra for over $550 (including tax) and have
to lug them around and dispose of them afterward?
This didn't make sense to me, when we could rent
them for so much less, and have them delivered and
picked up.

Wrong again! When I expressed my concern (okay,
outrage) at buying six candelabra, the Bride provided
me with a list of numbers of rent-it centers in the
Manhattan area. I started making calls. Most of them
didn't have silver candelabra at all. Those that did had
only one or two. Finally, I found one that had the
requisite six silver candelabra and would be willing to
rent, deliver to, and pick them up from the wedding
site…all for a mere $780. Wait, I think there was tax
on top of that.

Suddenly the Pier One candelabra began to look very
good! However, when we reached NYC on August 27,
I discovered that the Bride had still not managed to

buy the candelabra. No problem—we had the van so we'd just go pick them up.

Except that all of them had been sold. We called all the other branches in Manhattan, and none of them had any either. It seems some other bride had been very busy!

Back to square one. Forgetting my initial reluctance, I now wanted those candelabra, and nothing was going to stop me from having them. After driving home from NYC today, calling a multitude of stores in CP, harassing a number of salespeople, and driving some 90 additional miles to three different stores, we finally managed to collect six of the same candelabra. Could we fit them in our laundry room staging area until they could be transported to NYC? No, they'd better join the candles in the basement. Although the Bride optimistically pointed out that maybe she could sell them afterwards, I'm a bit amazed that I not only agreed to, but actively participated in this mad scheme.

Hotel reservations, or lack thereof. August 31.

Since the Bride and Groom lived only a few blocks from the Gramercy Park Hotel, where the bulk of the wedding rooms had been reserved, the FOB and I decided yesterday to take a peek at a suite to make sure it would be big enough for the Bride and us.

Unfortunately, we didn't make it that far, because the hotel didn't seem to have a record of our reservation.

What a nightmare! With a sinking feeling, I requested a printout of all our guests' reservations, and found other names missing from the list. No, the Front Desk could not make the reservation again; the Special Events Coordinator would have to do that. No, unfortunately, she had already gone for the day. (It was before noon.)

Infuriated, I called again this morning from CP. The Coordinator must have been taking her siesta, so I left a voicemail. No return call. Well, the MOB will not go quietly. I called again and again, until I finally got through to her. She couldn't figure out what could have happened, but she did mention that there was another wedding party by the same name and wondered if our reservation could have been deleted with theirs. She made another reservation, but my confidence is badly shaken.

Will we in fact have a place to lay our heads for the wedding weekend, or should we stake out a street corner?

WORK AND PLAY IN CENTRAL PA

Early September

Heading home. September 5.

One of my mother's best friends was sweet enough to have an engagement party for us at her house in CP. Since the invitations would be back from the printers, we had decided to do them the same weekend. Finally my mother will get to put her newfound calligraphy skills to work!

The engagement gift. September 5.

Nothing is easy! I had been looking for a really special engagement gift for the Bride and Groom. I wanted something that had some tradition to it and would be a "keeper" for the future, so I checked into various cultural traditions. The FOB being a die-hard Irishman, I considered, very briefly, the Irish tradition of giving a horseshoe, and found it lacking in appeal. My cultural background, on the other hand, is French. All right, only one quarter French, but that was quite enough to justify the giving of a *Coupe de Mariage*, which is a lovely French tradition. It is a two-handled silver cup, which has the initials of the couple and the date of the marriage engraved on it, and is traditionally used by the couple to drink their first toast after they are married.

After much searching, I finally located an Internet site that had a Wedding Cup. Although they promised to deliver before the date of the engagement party, September 7, I had not received it by today. I called to inquire. For some reason it had not yet been engraved, so they had to overnight it to me without the engraving so that it could be presented at the party. I then would have to send it back to them for engraving later. It wasn't totally satisfactory, but it was the best they could do. Don't ever believe that a promised item will reach you on time! Call, call back, and call again to check on the progress.

The invitations. September 7.

I've noticed a disturbing trend since I got engaged: I've become a little...flighty. I often find myself incapable of focusing on a task at hand because I'm so busy thinking about the other 27 things I have to do.

Which is why I shouldn't have been surprised that when I finished stuffing all the invitations, I mysteriously had one extra reply card envelope. I tried to hide it from my mother, who had kept urging me to concentrate instead of talk while we were doing them, but the more I tried to figure it out, the more confused I got.

Finally, we decided to unstuff all 100 envelopes to figure out what went wrong. Amazingly, not only had I screwed up the stuffing—forgetting to put a reply card envelope in one invitation—but I had also misnumbered the reply card envelopes (our system for tracking who had and hadn't responded), and there were two #14's. My mother could only shake her head, a look of complete dismay on her face.

The invitations. September 7.

As much as I wanted some "bonding" time while we were doing the invitations, I knew we wouldn't be able to converse without messing up. Of course, my darling daughter didn't listen. And once again the MOB is right! I just wish we didn't have to spend two extra hours doing invitations to prove it.

The engagement party. September 7.

Fun! The Bride and Groom seemed delighted with the *Coupe de Mariage*, despite the absence of the engraving at this point. Hopefully it will be passed on to future generations.

The evening was also "instructional" for the Bride and Groom. It was calculated that among the guests there were well in excess of 250 years of marriage, so we decided to shower advice on the Bride and Groom in addition to gifts. All attendees wrote a piece of advice on a blank piece of paper without signing their names. The Bride, who knew the guests much better than the Groom, read the advice and reacted to it; then they had to guess who had written it. Some was funny and some was serious. Mine was much too easy, since my advice was: "Move to Central PA." I wonder how she knew it was me? And did she know that mine was really serious? NYC seems so far away!

PREPARATIONS REACH A FEVERISH PITCH

September–October

The queen of returns. September 9.

About a month ago my husband awarded me this title, which is not without some validity. I more than deserved it today! I'm relatively sure that I return fewer items than I keep, but the margin of difference is not too great. Today, after getting the invitations into the mail and sending the *Coupe de Mariage* for engraving, I began my returns for the day:

1) a Unity candle which the Bride didn't like since it had gold print on it. I knew she wouldn't like it—why did I buy it?
2) three lace collars that I had bought to decorate the flower girl baskets, but which looked terrible!

3) clear address labels, because we decided that hand addressing (even with my bad calligraphy) was preferable to script labels on the computer.
4) an oval basket I had bought as a "necessities basket" for the ladies room, since the Groom's mother had one already.

To be fair, this was a larger return day than usual since I had been buying items and saving them to show to the Bride over the weekend for her approval or disapproval. In retrospect, the second of these categories won out.

On the plus side, I found a sale on pillar candles and bought enough for the six candelabra. I also went to a candle factory and bought a Unity candle with two matching tapers, plain white and simply carved. I had seen this set a few days before and described it to the Bride, who proclaimed it perfect. Let's hope so, since the factory accepts no returns. Do you think they heard about me before I got there?

To top off the Returns Extravaganza, I got a call from the Bride tonight. The Bride, after enlisting my help to buy some place settings of her casual china pattern locally, realized that it chipped easily. Now I will have the opportunity to return these items, too!

The princess of returns. September 9.

Okay, maybe I did tell her that I'd trust her judgment in choosing items. I'm tempted to feel bad about making her return so many things. But isn't a mother supposed to know what you wanted, without your having to say it...even if you previously, unthinkingly, told her the opposite?

A mental note. September 10.

Every now and then I must remind myself of the motto of this wedding: "The Bride is Always Right." It's helpful to repeat this to myself at frequent intervals and any time I'm tempted to disagree with one of her ideas. It's not easy with the close relationship we have, since

I find it hard not to speak my mind. However, remembering this motto helps me to conclude any adverse remark by saying, "Of course, it's your wedding and your decision." And of course, I mean it, because I want her to be happy!

Preparing for the great event.
September 10.

For the past six weeks, I've been working out with a personal trainer. Now before you give me grief about my wedding budget, let me just explain that this is not for the wedding. My personal training sessions have

been budgeted under the more accurate heading of "Event-Unrelated Personal Health and Wellness." They just happened to coincide with the two months before my wedding, and may mysteriously end just about the time I start my honeymoon. Any more questions?

Anyway, I'm having a really difficult time losing weight. It's never been hard for me to drop pounds before just by eating a little less and stepping up the exercise. But for some reason, it's not happening. I'm wondering if it has something to do with how I deal with stress. While I hear of other brides losing their appetite merely thinking about the big day, stress just makes me reach for a maple scone (which I've recently taken to microwaving for exactly 20 seconds so the maple nuggets melt slightly—so scrumptious). My first fitting is in a couple weeks and I really want to be down a few pounds. My trainer has been great, sending me threatening emails at work and generally punishing me twice a week, but I need more. I resolve to limit myself to 1000 calories a day and cut out the egg and cheese bagels, which have recently replaced my normal breakfast routine of yogurt and cereal.

<u>Preparing for the great event.</u>
<u>September 10.</u>

I just can't lose weight! I've been exercising on the treadmill and swimming 40 to 60 laps a day but the scale keeps hovering around the same ugly number. I feel more toned, and clothes are a little looser, but the weight just won't drop off the way it used to. Moral of the story: Make sure your daughter gets married before you turn 60.

How else can I prepare? A few years ago, my daughter (before she became The Bride) suggested I get my teeth bleached. I resisted for any number of reasons, none of them memorable, but which seemed valid at the time. In June of this year, I decided I would get them bleached for the wedding. I went through the three-week process with some degree of success and saved two tubes of bleach for a "touch-up" nearer the event. Will reapply in early October so I can dazzle them with my pearly whites!

Hair appointments have been scheduled so that I'll have a perm, color and a cut all just a few weeks before the wedding. I'll be holding my breath until I'm sure all these processes are successful.

And a joint preparation for the FOB and me: Although my husband and I can perform adequately on the dance floor, I've always wished we could do better. Over the years I've asked him several times if he would take dancing lessons with me. I've had a lifelong love affair with the waltz, which looks so elegant and graceful, and I've always wanted to learn how to do it. Well, a few weeks ago, I asked FOB if we could take some ballroom dancing lessons in preparation for the wedding and he said YES! I checked some local studios, found one that had just started a Beginners'

Ballroom course, and last week we joined the group for their second lesson. I'm convinced that if we practice, we can do this.

Mounting stress. September 10.

Today I received some helpful phone calls:

1:37 p.m. A bridesmaid informing me she has received a "made to her measurements" dress that is approximately four sizes too large.

2:04 p.m. The mother of two flower girls asking if I can handle selecting, picking up and mailing their dresses because the woman who answers the phone speaks only Spanish and their online ordering system is broken.

2:24 p.m. Another bridesmaid indicating she has just received a dress so low-cut she fears she will be mistaken for a stripper.

I carried it off with composure: I walked outside my building, plopped down on a bench and started crying hysterically. I immediately called my mom but she couldn't understand what I was saying. Most people in the immediate vicinity were staring, but some came over and gently offered a tissue or a comforting pat. None of it mattered—I was filled with self-righteous indignation: "I am the Bride, and I do not deserve this! I went to great lengths to find cute bridesmaid and flower girl dresses that didn't cost a fortune, and this is the thanks I get?" Somewhere in the back of my mind the phrase "you get what you pay for" was playing. Maybe I should have paid more just for peace of mind?

My mother was her usual rock of support, repeating how I could handle this and generally being her normal, well-adjusted self. What in the world would I do without her?

The bride melts down. September 10.

Got a call from the Bride tonight and it sounds as though things are really getting to her. This is a stressful time at best, but when several things go wrong at once, it's tough to take. Work sounds impossibly busy, with no time to make necessary phone calls for wedding preparations. There are problems with how and where to accommodate the six children at the reception. Her friends, who come from many different geographic locations, are calling her to ask when the bachelorette party will be, but it appears not to be finalized as yet. It's a tough situation for the Bride since it's completely out of her hands.

When the Bride gets upset, it's the MOB's job to be calm, no matter how upset she really feels. Of course, my immediate reaction is to go to battle for my "chick" and fix everything, but nothing I can do will solve these problems. So I attempt to be rational and explain that "these are really not insurmountable problems; they just seem that way because they're all hitting you at once."

And: "This will all work out; just give it time."

No improvement? Okay, let's try: "Some things are just out of your control, so you do everything you can to control what you can and then must just accept that there are things you cannot control." My best advice always seems inadequate when my daughter is feeling down. Usually, after this much reassurance, she starts to come around. Not this time—this must really be a serious meltdown.

Still no improvement. September 12.

Got an email from the Bride, saying she is still upset. Sent more advice, the same advice I've given her all her life: "Try to step back and put it in perspective. Try focusing on what's good and positive…like the fact that you are marrying the man you love and that you will have a wonderful life together. If you look at the big picture, the other problems seem less important."

Random thoughts. September 13.

Lately I've been thinking a lot about my maternal grandmother. She died when my mother was 13, a fact my mother probably still hasn't gotten completely over. I wonder if my grandmother is watching me, wondering how her perfectly sane, well-adjusted daughter could have produced such a lunatic. Hopefully she laughs rather than cries watching me lose it on a park bench. My mother talks so fondly about her—about how sweet and supportive she was— and I find myself wishing for the millionth time that I had known her.

Recently, though, the longing is mixed with a strange realization: that my mother went through this entire crazy wedding-planning process without her mother. I wonder how in the world she got through it. The thought of it makes me really sad, and I realize for the thousandth time how lucky I am to have such a wonderful mother, especially now. I hope she knows that I intend to make it up to her with very well-behaved, adoring grandchildren.

Who is this girl? September 13.

Somehow the daughter I remember, who was always so sweet and reasonable, so considerate and reliable, has disappeared. She has been replaced by a creature so focused on fondant colors and menu layouts, it's as if the outside world doesn't exist.

Okay, there *were* a few episodes in her youth that foreshadowed this tunnel vision. This is the girl who announced the day she got her driver's license that she "had decided that she would never have an accident."

95

As if stating it could make it come true. You guessed it—in the first week after she got her license, she had an "encounter" with a white pick-up truck.

And then there was her senior year in high school, when the stress and uncertainty of waiting for college acceptance turned her into an unrecognizable individual. All right, there's precedent for this extraordinary behavior, and an excuse as well—after all, she's the Bride.

The dresses—Again. September 14.

Three days of nonstop 'friends and family' therapy and I'm practically back to my old self. Yes, the world can start turning again, and there is light at the end of my broken-down tunnel.

I was reveling in the glory of Saturday morning waffles and looking forward to a blissful day of wedding-march music evaluation when the phone rang:

"Sheila? It's Rachel, your sister-in-law to be."

"Hi! I know who you are. You're the only Rachel in my life. Please tell me you're calling just to chat."

"Well...not really. Unfortunately, there's a small, actually just teensy-weensy problem."

I stopped chewing. Waffle stuck in the back of my mouth. "Uh oh. What is it?"

"Your dressmaker? She's completely crazy."

My heart sank. I knew it was too good to be true. After Jenine and Mindy called the other day with their disastrous experiences, I had called my dressmaker, who assured me that she had accidentally sent the wrong dresses to just two of my bridesmaids. She had guaranteed that the measurements were right on the others, and that there would be no more problems. She had promised to mail the correct dresses to Jenine and Mindy the following day, and I had hung up feeling much better.

Until now. I sighed deeply.

"What happened?"

"Well, I wasn't going to tell you this, but last week she sent me a dress that was just a little too small at the bust line. Actually, I couldn't get it below my neck. When I called, she said she'd made a mistake and would mail me the right dress the next day."

I bit my lip to keep from screaming.

"So I decided that instead of risking another mistake, I would drive into the city and pick it up myself."

"Okay, so it worked out then?"

"Well, actually I went to her shop and picked it up and was halfway down the block with it when she came running after me, yelling that she had given me the wrong one again. The one she gave me was actually for Rebecca, so I took them both, and stopped by Rebecca's apartment and dropped hers off."

Rebecca was another of Gary's sisters. She lived at Astor Place, just a couple blocks from Gary and me.

"Except that the dress she gave me for Rebecca didn't fit her either."

That was it. I lost it. The whole world was going to hear it about my stupid dressmaker, especially poor Rachel, who was just the messenger.

"Well, you want to know why that happened, Rachel? You really want to know? I'll tell you why. Because she's a FREAKING IDIOT!"

"Honestly, it's no big deal. I didn't want to stress you out, but I wanted you to know that she's pretty flaky, in case other people had problems."

"Yes, that's very helpful. Jenine especially will be grateful to know that's why she looks like an exotic dancer in her dress." I had started whimpering, and I could tell Rachel was getting panicked.

"Like I said, it's no big deal. This will be FINE, ok? Rebecca and I will sort it out, and if I need to drive

*into the city five times to make sure the dress fits, I
will. Okay? Sheila?"*

*I couldn't take it anymore. I gave the phone to Gary in
desperation. While I blared Vivaldi's Four Seasons, I
heard him in the background yelling "I TOLD you not
to tell her!"*

Plans for the bridal shower.
September 17.

Emails whizzed back and forth about the bridal
shower. It's to be held in an Italian restaurant in the
DC area. I wanted to help and volunteered to think
about favors to go along with the Italian theme. The
Maid of Honor called, and I mentioned a brainstorm
about the favors. I had been trying to think of some
breakaway centerpieces that could be used as favors as
well. Eyeing the basil from my herb garden, I thought
how darling it would look to have little pots of various
herbs in large baskets lined with red and white checked
cloths. Bright and colorful, perfect for the Italian
theme, and useful for anyone who cooks. She liked the
idea, so I said I would work on it.

Of course, I couldn't let well enough alone. I had to
paint the pots as well. Wouldn't they be cute if they
had the Bride's and Groom's names and the wedding
date? And a tag with clever information too? I really
got into it with stars, checks, hearts, flowers, and
ladybugs in white paint with touches of black and red

detailing. They looked great! Oops! I touched one with a damp hand and the black ink smudged. This was supposed to be waterproof! I couldn't take it any more and went to bed.

This morning at 6:45 a.m., I couldn't sleep because I was thinking about the dumb pots! So I got up and redid them. I am so over these pots! I can't believe I still have two more steps to do before they're done.

Tiaras and tire marks. September 21.

I woke up determined that this *Saturday would be different. I would give myself a break and focus on just one item of my to-do list. No problems, no dramas, just me at the Bridal Building, picking out my tiara. Eight hours of stress-free shopping stretched out in front of me.*

Ah, the Bridal Building. That oasis of wedding bargains smack in the middle of Manhattan. Wonder of wonders, they actually sell tiaras for less than $900.

I took the subway and got off at Herald Square. Passing by Macy's, I was struck by what a beautiful day it was. The sun was shining; the sky was so blue... wait, were those wedding shoes *on that store-front mannequin? Does Macy's carry wedding shoes? I need wedding shoes, but I don't think that style would look good on me...maybe something with a higher heel...*

"WATCH OUT!"

In a daze, I turn in the direction of the voice. Before I can react, I feel myself being lifted up into the air, and I see my brand-new red Steve Madden shoes go flying off my feet and into the sky above me. I land with a thud on the pavement below, my shoes raining down on top of me.

That's right: Four screwed-up bridesmaids dresses, a truckload of lost hotel reservations and honeymooning with a tribe of cannibals weren't enough.

I had been hit by a high-speed bicyclist.

Bewildered, I looked around. People were starting to gather. I felt someone helping me up and heard voices asking if I was okay. My head was spinning, but I appeared alive. I nodded, trying to figure out how on earth this could have happened. Why didn't I see him? Did I step out into the street without looking both ways? I couldn't believe I had been so stupid. Unbelievably, the cyclist, upon determining that I was not in need of immediate CPR, proceeded to pedal off into the distance.

I looked down and noticed that my knee and elbow were skinned and bleeding. Even more disturbing, my left hand—which I had used to break my fall— appeared to be spurting copious amounts of blood. The same hand, I might add, that everyone will be looking at when Gary slips a ring on it in exactly 6 weeks.

As my head began to clear, it hit me: Broadway goes only one way, and I had looked in the direction of oncoming traffic to make sure the coast was clear before I crossed. I didn't see the bicyclist because he was coming from the wrong direction! It was his fault! How dare he ruin my tiara-shopping and pristine ring hand!

Luckily, the offending party was stuck at a red light. I slipped my shoes back on, broke through the crowd and bolted after him.

"Excuse me, sir? I couldn't help but notice that you were cycling against traffic, which is illegal. If you had been cycling in the proper direction, the accident could have been avoided, because I would have seen you before I crossed the street. Next time you should make sure you cycle with traffic." Yes, that was some self-restraint I was exercising. All those bridal etiquette books must be working—I was the very model of courtesy!

The cyclist looked at me like I'd just asked him to bicycle naked. "Yeah, well, it happens honey. I'm sorry you got hit but that's how it goes."

I stared at him with my mouth agape as every ounce of sanity drained from my body. I could feel the blood pulsing faster out of my hand as I fought to keep from strangling him.

"It happens when IDIOTS like you don't obey traffic laws! Not to mention that there's a good chance I'll have to get MARRIED in six weeks wrapped in gauze because of you! You will pay—mark my words—YOU WILL PAY!"'

Frantically, I tried to flag down a passing policeman to write him a ticket, but none appeared. In the middle of my tirade the light turned green, and he pedaled off.

I was still screaming when I noticed a cook from Angelo's Pizza across the street was tentatively waving Betadyne and a large strip of gauze at me.

Daily rituals. September 21.

If you find your mail boring, plan a wedding! It's always exciting to see what the mail brings each day. As soon as it arrives, I sit down to record acceptances and regrets. And try to figure out what some of the guests mean by their responses. Apparently, our response cards were not as straightforward as I thought.

Of course, nothing about my life is boring these days, with the Bride agonizing over her crazy dressmaker, and suffering from a remarkably bizarre encounter with a bicycle. Just when I thought I had a reliable stable of 'keep your chin up' platitudes, I have to develop one for a post-traumatic pedestrian-meets-cyclist event. What will happen next?

Overlays are still coming along, and I've become the great improviser, using tuna cans to hold the slippery material in place! (This is less fattening than eating the tuna mixed with gobs of mayo.) Listening to books on tape makes the whole experience less painful. Up to date with 14 overlays completed.

FOB and I have continued to attend our weekly dance class, and I think we're getting better. Of course, our improvement depends on how much we practice, and it is not quite the daily ritual it should be. The U-shaped counter that divides the kitchen and family room has a tendency to impede our steps, which makes practice frustrating. (Not to mention the fact that we don't always agree about the proper way to execute the steps.) But dancing at our daughter's wedding will make it all worthwhile.

The overlays—and then some. *September 25.*

My mother has informed me that she has completed all the overlays—20 large and 10 small. She is truly amazing, and I am filled with customary inadequacy: My daughter will have to wear store-bought Halloween costumes! Before I can bask in the relief of another task completed, she informs me that she has a tremendous amount of leftover silver-gray organza.

That's perfect! I'll use it to stuff the gift boxes for my bridesmaids and flower girls.

But wait, she's still talking. It seems the size of the fabric remnants is just the perfect width for bridesmaids' wraps, which she also plans to make.

Before I can reflect on the image of my bridesmaids matching the overlays on each table, my mother moves on to describe her vision for me. There is also just enough fabric for her to make a long sweeping cape for over my dress—a fairy-tale princess kind of shimmering cape—with a hood that would fall back over my shoulders. She further announces that when the bridal party is introduced at the reception, the bridesmaids could enter wearing their wraps, and I could wear the cape!

My mind is whirling. Which silver-gray issue to tackle first? Suddenly, I remember. My gown already comes with a matching wrap! My mother takes that one well, but the bridesmaids are trickier. I don't want to hurt my mother's feelings, especially after all she's done. In the end, I decide to be honest: I'm sure the bridesmaids would like the wraps for New Years Eve or some other "glitzy" occasion, but I don't know how they would feel about making an entrance matching the tablecloths.

Say goodbye to the silver cape.
September 25.

There was a definite hesitation when I suggested that silver-gray shimmering cape to her. Guess I got a little carried away. Wonder if the paint fumes from the pots got to my head?

Trouble sleeping. September 26.

I woke up in the middle of the night last night and couldn't get back to sleep. This has been a rather frequent occurrence recently, because once I wake up, I can't stop thinking about all the things that still need to be done, and wondering what we will forget to do. I keep a notepad and flashlight by the side of the bed, so I can jot down my concerns; then the next morning I try to resolve all the previous night's issues so I won't worry about them the next night.

Last night I was remembering how I always used to worry that I would cry too much when my daughter was married. I still think I'll cry, but at this point, I'm thinking that they'll be tears of joy, not only for her happiness, but because the planning process (and worrying) is over!

I called my friend, the bridal company owner, today to alert him that I still had not received my MOB gown, which he was going to mail to me. It appears he has the dress, but just hadn't gotten around to mailing it. I've learned my lesson: If I have not received an ordered item a week before its expected arrival, call immediately!

I think I need a break. My college roommate is arriving tomorrow for a long weekend. Since we haven't seen each other for about ten years, we will probably talk and laugh ourselves hoarse. I wish someone had told me to schedule in regular breaks from all the wedding planning—whenever I've taken even just a day off from all of this, I've always felt so rejuvenated.

Trouble sleeping. September 29.

The stress of a budget florist superimposed on the general anxiety of wedding planning provided an interesting dream sequence last night: I was standing at the opening of the ceremony, ready to walk down the aisle, when I noticed my mother had disappeared.

Everyone was making strange excuses for her ("She went to feed the dog; she'll be back soon."), but eventually I got suspicious. Finally, a bridesmaid nervously confessed that, the florist hadn't shown up, and my mother was out trying to find me a bouquet.

Just then my mother burst through the front door of the church (for some strange reason she was wearing a long, silver-gray organza cape) carrying a large assortment of long-stemmed red roses. Which would have been great except every stem was bent at a 45-degree angle halfway down the stem. My mother announced that every flower shop in town was closed, she had found these at the Food Emporium, and that if I simply angled my arms like so, no one would notice.

As if on cue, the music started playing, my mother thrust the mutant roses into my arms, and I was so touched I started crying. And that's when I woke up.

Pre-wedding stress dream, or eerie premonition?

I'm getting nervous. October 10.

No, not about the day itself, just about the preparations. Being a former teacher, I'm used to planning in advance and controlling those plans. It's very difficult that there are so many things I cannot do—like, for example, the wedding program, since the Bride and Groom have yet to decide on their music and readings. I know I've got to leave things like the processional and recessional to the Bride and Groom but every time I ask if they're done, the answer is no. Reminder: Don't be a control freak.

Then there's the band. Since I haven't spoken with them myself, I don't know whether everything is all set or not. And the favors seem to be hanging fire. Things that are left until the last minute make me really nervous. I don't want to be a nag. I'm sure they'll get it done. Or will they?

The honeymoon (Round III). October 10.

Gary arrived home tonight looking despondent. He quietly informed me in his "serious voice" that I needed to steel myself—he has some really bad news.

It appears that it is now too unsafe to go to Guyana for our honeymoon. The previous baseline level of general unrest has escalated significantly—the "new" unrest is characterized by daylight assassinations.

I managed to suppress the urge to drop to my knees and sob with relief. Instead, I gave him a big hug and tried to focus on how disappointed he was. This made me sad, so I was able to keep from grinning broadly. Not that I was not looking forward to Guyana. Under ordinary circumstances, I'm as adventurous as they come, and would love to take a vacation there. It's just that the stress and non-stop action of this wedding planning has actually led me to crave an all-inclusive resort—once a bad word in my vocabulary—that caters to exhausted newlyweds, in a country that doesn't require immunizations. I conveyed this to Gary, and he looked a little disappointed: "Oh, I was thinking maybe we could charter a boat for a week in the Caribbean instead." Gulp. (I hadn't realized I was marrying such an adventurer.) In short order, however, I've convinced him that tennis courts, frozen drinks with umbrellas, and cheesy Lovers' Raft Races are exactly what we need.

But exactly how are we going to plan that in the next two weeks?

The final fitting. October 15.

This is the most beautiful dress ever! It fits like a glove and shows off my newly-acquired back muscles (courtesy of my personal trainer). The beading is especially perfect: It reminds me of a 50's movie star. And I'm so glad I went with an A-line; it's timeless and classic. Gary is going to flip when he sees me. Tearfully I hug Giselle and thank her for finding my dress. And let's hear it for gown power-shopping!

Trauma. October 23.

Note the number of days without entries. I've been so upset that I've barely been able to function, let alone write about what is going on. In retrospect, it was a really stupid decision to have laser surgery to remove some facial lines just three weeks before the wedding.

On the other hand, the plastic surgeon that had recommended the procedure was aware of my timeline and had assured me there would be no problem.

No problem? Immediately after the surgery, I developed a black spot larger than a quarter on my right cheek.

Now I avert my eyes when I go into a room with a mirror. On our wedding anniversary, I refused to go out to dinner because I couldn't bear for anyone to see the way I looked. FOB has had quite a lot to put up with.

Calls and visits to the surgeon's office have elicited the information that I "must have extremely sensitive skin." That's true—I stressed that to him before the surgery. I can tell he's worried about a lawsuit. He assures me that it is healing. I can only hope that the next several days will do the trick so I will be presentable by Friday night's Rehearsal Dinner, and of course for the wedding.

First aid. October 24.

I'd sensed that she was distracted. She didn't even seem rightfully outraged when I told her our band refused to play any Gypsy Kings songs, which I'd always dreamed of having at my wedding. The nerve of them!

After I kept asking what was wrong, she finally let it slip. She felt terribly disfigured, not to mention betrayed by her doctor. I couldn't blame her. And I also couldn't believe she'd been suffering like this for the past week, and hadn't told me.

It kind of made my relentless agonizing over the dime-sized, practically healed cycling injury on my left palm seem, well, trivial.

Now it was my turn to do the comforting. Except that everything I said sounded so phony! If I had been going through this, I would have been inconsolable. I finally realized that nothing I said could make a difference, and—even worse—I was simply drawing attention to a topic she was trying to forget. I felt so helpless.

The video—A study in clandestine activity. October 27.

Thank goodness I've had a project to distract me from feeling sorry for myself.

Several months ago, the FOB had suggested that we do a video of the Bride's and Groom's lives for presentation at the Rehearsal Dinner. I received that suggestion enthusiastically, albeit with the reservations of someone who is technologically challenged. My husband assured me that his former assistant would help us put it together if we just collected the materials and wrote the captions. We further decided that it would be nice if the presentation could be a surprise.

Thus began a long campaign of surreptitiously finding pictures of the Bride and Groom during various periods of their lives. This was not as easy as you might think. The MOG told me that with five children, they didn't do much picture taking by the time the fourth one arrived, but came through with about 20 pictures of the Groom and their family.

Next, the FOB and I spent hours reviewing thousands of pictures we had taken over the years of the Bride's childhood. I also scavenged her room and found pictures from her college years, trips abroad and graduate school. (I didn't even feel guilty about snooping!) We selected those that corresponded best to the pictures we had of the Groom.

We still needed more pictures of the Groom. Enter the Best Men (to be), who were a terrific resource for embarrassing pictures of the Groom from college years forward. Another problem solved!

The dining room table, which had shortly before been released from its overlay captivity, became the base of operations and the caption writing began, a joint project of the POB. The BOB suggested music to accompany each section of the video. We turned over our 150 plus numbered pictures and captions to the FOB's former assistant, who worked her magic on them. We saw the final version today, and it's fantastic! This was a definite bright spot in an otherwise dark couple of weeks.

We've decided to show the video at the Rehearsal Dinner, and at the wedding reception as well. With as much time as we've spent on it, it should be required viewing for every guest. Next problem: How are we going to show it, and how will we get all the equipment we need up to NYC?

Obsessing over the weather.
October 28.

Two weeks before your wedding, the only site more interesting than TheKnot.com is WeatherChannel.com.

Against my videographer's advice to look only at the three-day forecast, I began a daily ritual of scanning the predictions at work. Which quickly became an hourly ritual, further reduced to every fifteen minutes, plus whenever I came back from the bathroom. The current assessment? It seems The Perfect Storm has formed over most of Manhattan for the nights of the rehearsal dinner and wedding. (Immediately before and afterwards, Earth returns to normal early-November weather of 0-.4 percent chance of precipitation.)

In short order, everyone I know has heard the news and is assigned another weather site to watch in the event of conflicting information. The updates flow in, but they are agonizingly consistent. Images of frizzy hair (mine) and empty ceremony seats (my guests') fill my head. There are no cabs to be had when it rains in Manhattan—how in the world are people going to get to and from the wedding?

114

I plead with God. After all, it poured at my high school graduation—shouldn't that count for something? And He knows there is nothing more precious than the pre-ceremony pictures of Gary and me outside, silhouetted against the Manhattan skyline. Finally, after 10 days of watching, the predictions become more dire ("wind gusts" morphing to "gale force"), I ask my mother to look into renting buses for everyone. What's another $800 at this point?

A contingency plan. October 29.

Bad news from the TV Weather Channel. We've been consulting it every hour or so, hoping it will change, but the bad news remains the same—high winds and rain, possibly snow for the wedding day. The Bride has always said that if it rains, it's impossible to get taxis. What to do?

Today I called every bus company in NYC, gathering information on costs and availability. The best deal was for a 20-passenger bus to take our guests to the wedding by ferrying back and forth between the hotel and the wedding site. Of course this would mean that some guests would have to leave extremely early in order for everyone to be accommodated. Since this bus is still available, we can wait till later on in the week to make a decision. Let's hope the weather report improves.

The honeymoon (Round IV).
October 29.

After spending most of the past week scouring Caribbean websites and calling travel agents, Gary announced that our honeymoon redo has been booked.

Since we were flying to Barbados already en route to Guyana, we decided to spend a week there, and another in nearby St. Lucia.

As relieved as I was that it was set, all this unexpected last-minute planning swallowed up the time Gary had planned to spend finishing his wedding "assignments"—burning the CD's of the "musical journey" of our relationship which we planned to give out as favors and doing other last-minute items.

Exhausted, we both stared at the mountain of CD labels, plastic cases and inserts, and collapsed. When would it ever get done?

Another decision not to decide.
October 30.

The forecast is still not wonderful, but the prospects of gale force winds and driving rain have lessened slightly. Guess we'll wait another day before deciding anything about the bus. I'll take the limousine company contact name and number to NYC with me in case the weather still looks really bad for Saturday.

THE COUNTDOWN BEGINS

October 31–

November 1

Insomniac. October 31. 5:30 a.m.

Staring at the ceiling, I made a mental list of the things I was stressing about:

1. *Universally mis-sized and ill-fitting bridesmaid's gowns will look like either minidresses or burkhas*
2. *Florist, if he even shows up, will forget to deliver candelabra, and will provide centerpieces in a lovely shade of magenta*
3. *Torrential downpour over next 72 hours will turn streets of New York into giant wading pool*

I suddenly realized I hadn't checked the Weather Channel in almost six hours! I raced to the living room, and paced anxiously while they endlessly dissected the impact of the New Mexico drought on the lizard population. Finally, the familiar sounds of "Your Local Weather" arrived. I assumed a yoga pose on the floor for a little extra zen, and tightly closed my eyes.

Strangely enough, I heard the meteorologist's voice piping in light and mellifluous...like when there's good news to report. I slowly opened one eye and, entirely prepared to wince, saw pictures of a sun for Friday, Saturday and Sunday on the five-day forecast! Okay, they were mostly obscured by clouds, but there were no angry lightning marks or rain marring the pictogram. In the distance, I heard the announcer saying the storm of the century was forming more slowly than expected, and was forecast to hit New England instead of the Mid-Atlantic region over the weekend.

Hooray! I jumped up and down and started yelling. I woke Gary up as well so he could share in the joy, but he was slightly less overcome.

Arrival day in the Big Apple. October 31.

With the entire contents of the "Wedding Staging Area and Adjunct" (formerly known as the laundry room and basement) in our mini-van, we arrived in NYC. Fortunately, our initial stops—at the Rehearsal Dinner site to drop off the video equipment and at the hotel to check in—went smoothly.

Next stop, the Bride's apartment. Thankfully, our son, who had just arrived from Denver, was waiting outside with a dolly full of things that had to go to the wedding site. We loaded them into the van and went upstairs to the apartment to see what else had to go, optimistic that we could take it all in one load. Think again. The apartment was full of boxes…and boxes…and boxes. Favors, cameras, liquor, gift bags, an endless array of baskets—where did we get all this stuff? The only thing missing was the Bride, who was supposed to help transport it.

Uh-oh. Emergency phone call from the Bride—she's stuck at work? Don't they know she's getting married in 48 hours? Poor thing. She must be so frustrated!

Sans the Bride, we managed to get everything down to the reception site in only two trips. We filled up a huge closet with all the wedding effects. I made a mental note of gratitude that the reception site provided such a large and lockable area for it all.

Career and wedding—they don't mix. October 31.

Nothing will test your career more than planning a wedding. Early on, I vowed that I would not become

121

the vacant bride who does nothing but plan her wedding at work. For the past six months, I've continued to work 60-hour weeks at work, skipping lunch, and doing minimal work on my wedding during the hours of 8 a.m. to 8 p.m. (all to the great dismay of my mother, who was burdened with all the weekday grunt work).

Which is why I felt more than justified asking for a day and a half off before my wedding. My parents were coming into town and needed my help dropping off the myriad of items at the reception site. I arrived at work extra early and planned to leave by noon.

Surprise! At 11:15 a.m., my boss—with whom I share an office—casually remarked that she needed me to complete some slides for an upcoming Board presentation before I left.

She is out of her mind. Complete a polished deck of slides for our Board of Directors? That will take at least two hours! Is this how she repays my loyalty? Surely if I appeared strikingly panicked about my ability to complete this momentous task given my "competing priorities," she would back off. I gave her my best deer-in-the-headlights look and grudgingly said I would do the best I could. To my astonishment, she breezily thanked me and went on working.

At 12:30 my parents called to ask where I was. In a loud voice, I remarked that I had just gotten a last-minute project and that I probably wouldn't be able to leave for some time. I could tell my parents were annoyed—after all, I had told them I would be there, and they couldn't do it alone. My boss didn't catch this hint-of-hints either, instead emailing back a set of revisions to the first round of slides I had sent her. The most remarkable aspect of this scenario was that she herself had gotten married just a year earlier and hadn't even worked while planning her wedding!

At 2:15 p.m. I finally finished the slides and skated home—annoyed, anxious and totally stressed. My parents, with my brother's help, had already taken two trips to the reception site in nightmarish NYC traffic and looked like they were ready to collapse. Once again, I felt like a total Bridezilla.

The Bride arrives. October 31.

When the Bride finally arrived, we raced to the florist to drop off the candelabra and lattice board for decorating, and then rushed around buying 20 vases for the floral arrangements. (The Bride was supposed to buy them weeks earlier, but I resisted the urge to lecture about leaving things to the last minute.)

Next stop was the bridal salon where we picked up the pièce de resistance, the bridal gown, freshly ironed and carefully placed into a protective bag with a multitude of tissues.

We now had a fifth "person" in our hotel suite. The gown took up residence in our living room, after we had followed strict orders to take it out of its bag and fluff it immediately. We hung it on the back of an open closet door, amazed at its capacity to billow out and fill the whole room.

I was certain that someone was going to step on it (and the BOB did, within just a few minutes, although the Bride never found out). We then covered all the edges with the tissue paper it had been packed in and resolved not to invite anyone to our suite. We would resist all urges for celebratory cocktail events and remain incommunicado! How did other POB have time to get together with friends before a wedding?

We're done! October 31. 6:00 p.m.

Had we really accomplished everything? The Bride had returned to her apartment to finish up a few tasks. FOB had retired to the bedroom to catch a quick nap. BOB had installed himself on the sofa, and we were quietly chatting. I remembered something I needed from my suitcase and walked into the darkened bedroom to find it.

I found it all right, with my left foot! I must have left the suitcase sticking out behind the bureau and it sent me flying. Pain shot up my leg as I pictured myself being walked down the aisle on crutches. I gingerly tested it out and could barely walk. Although it didn't

seem broken, it wasn't "danceable" either. I quickly
iced it and prayed that it would heal by the morning.

A little down time . October 31. 7:30 p.m.

*I can't believe I'm getting married in two days. I'm so
excited, but nervous at the same time that everything
will go right. The knot in my stomach is making it hard
to eat dinner. I need to chill out.*

*Wait! How could I have forgotten? It's Halloween—
one of my favorite days of the year! And a charity Gary
works with has a big party every year. Yes, that's just
what I need to forget about wedding stress and my
last-minute to-do list. We'll just stay long enough to
say hi to everyone and for me to relax a bit. Good
thing I have my bellydancing outfit handy.*

Planning ahead?
October 31. 8:00 p.m.

We had no sooner finished eating our Tibetan take-out
with the Bride and Groom and the BOB, when
suddenly the formerly stressed-out, overworked Bride
was putting on a Halloween costume! She seemed
oblivious to the fact that her bridesmaids' gifts weren't
wrapped, and 180 programs had yet to be folded. The
groom followed suit with a borrowed Robin Hood
costume and they were out the door. (They were
gracious enough to ask us to accompany them, but

even the BOB, normally a party animal, had the sense to refuse.) We went home to bed!

Somewhat behind schedule.
November 1. 11:02 a.m.

I am an idiot. After having a marvelous time at numerous Halloween parties, we finally arrived home at 2 a.m.

And woke up at 11 a.m. exhausted, the floor littered with wedding programs and silver gift boxes.

Now I was even more stressed out. Why did I go out last night? I didn't even win any of the costume prizes, even though I was the cutest bellydancer there.

Hopefully, the manicure, pedicure and massage I have planned for today will melt away all my stress.

Wedding Eve.
November 1.

The Bride became somewhat distraught this morning. She had planned to have a relaxing day today with just two appointments, but after a number of items came up, it was anything but relaxing. (I resisted the urge to remark that her Halloween night could have been better spent with last-minute preparations.)

One highlight of the day was the manicure/pedicure we had done together. How thoughtful of her! She wanted us to have some time alone together, and wanted to give me something that I wouldn't have given myself.

It was a wonderful idea, but there were problems. First, we got a late start. Next, there were no taxis to be found. So we rushed to the subway, and jumped on the train, only to find that we were going in the wrong direction—uptown, instead of downtown! (The Bride, after all, had only lived here for two and a half years.) We got off at the next stop, and once again had trouble finding a taxi.

At this point, the Bride broke into tears in the middle of Park Avenue. As I put my newly-perfected 'Bridal Meltdown' skills to work, a taxi magically appeared.

By now we were really late, and the Bride called the nail salon to be sure that we could be a little late for our appointment. No problem there, but the Bride's anxiety was mounting.

The manicures and pedicures were a wonderful experience. Some mother/daughter bonding time—I loved it! However, with our late start, the appointment ran over, which made her late for her next appointment—a massage. Stress again! Cell phone call again! Could she be a little late for her massage appointment? Yes, that would be okay. Relief again! After the massage, the Bride would stop by her apartment, get dressed for the Rehearsal Dinner, and pick up the things she needed to stay overnight with us before returning to the hotel.

Are all 21st century brides (and wedding preparations) this crazy?

Somewhat more behind schedule. November 1. 4:30 p.m.

Take it from me: No matter how well you plan, there will always be a million things that arise the day before your wedding and suck up all your precious time. Take the gift bags, for example. When I dropped them off at the Westin Times Square, they couldn't find the reservations of the guests staying there. A half-hour later they straightened it out, and then informed me I had to get the gift bags checked through security.

The problem: Security was on the other side of the hotel. What should have been a 15-minute errand took over an hour.

It didn't help that I was already two hours behind schedule and still hadn't folded the programs. My mother's advice not to let everything go till the last minute played like a broken record in my mind. Why didn't I listen to her?

The bridesmaids arrive.
November 1. 6:30 p.m.

When I got back to the hotel, I had plenty of time to get ready. This was the first time I had tried to cover the damaged area on my cheek. To my enormous relief, the spot had faded from black to a light red and I was able to camouflage it pretty well.

The Bride had arranged with her bridesmaids to come to our suite before the Rehearsal Dinner so she could give them their necklaces and matching earrings to go with their dresses. As they began to gather in our room, the Maid of Honor, who had just arrived from DC, expressed her concern about finding time the next day to get to the seamstress who had made her dress to have it altered.

What? I couldn't believe what I was hearing! The wedding was in less than 24 hours and her dress wasn't ready? Panicked, I asked what it was, and she said the hem needed to be shortened. Thinking she couldn't possibly get to and from the seamstress the day of the wedding, I said that I could probably do it, and the Maid of Honor said she would appreciate it.

One look at the Bride's face and I knew it was a mistake.

One last crisis. November 1. 6:30 p.m.

After a fast shower, I quickly wrapped the bridemaids' gifts and headed for the hotel. Shortly after, all eight of my bridesmaids arrived in my parents' suite and I handed out the gift boxes.

While we were chatting, my maid-of-honor let it slip that she hadn't had her dress altered yet.

I was mad. I couldn't direct it at her, since this dress was supposed to be "made to her (very petite) measurements," and it was perfect only for a size-two Amazon. (Astoundingly, the dressmaker had managed to screw up six out of the eight dresses.) Nevertheless, we had discussed this problem already, and she was going to come to NYC a day early and get it done. She then had to change her reservations because of work and didn't arrive until about two hours ago. Ahhh!

While my mind whirled, I heard my mother offer to hem it for her. My mother is always the first to help out when there's a problem, but I didn't want her hemming a dress the day of my wedding! I wanted her to relax and have time to get ready. But I also didn't want a bridesmaid with a hem down to her shoes. Why do these dilemmas always seem to happen to me?

I quickly intervened and said that my Maid of Honor would have to get an early-hour appointment with the dressmaker, or else find someone else to hem it. This being Manhattan, with tailors on every corner, it shouldn't be a problem.

Don't people know that only the Bride is allowed to procrastinate?

The Rehearsal Dinner. November 1. 7:00 p.m.

I had a wonderful time at the Rehearsal Dinner. The Bride and Groom have some terrific friends and it was such fun meeting them. Besides, once the video had been set up, the FOB and I didn't have any responsibilities to play host or hostess that night. We could just enjoy ourselves.

Sadly, I have to confess to yet another occasion of making a comment without thinking about it first. Two in one night—that's a record! One of the Bride's party, a former roommate, was a longtime favorite of mine.

She's one of those people who is always upbeat, very organized and willing to help. She had been very helpful with all kinds of wedding planning, and tonight offered assistance in yet another wedding matter. I responded with a hug and the comment that she was terrific and I wished I could have her for a daughter-in-law! The BOB, I've always believed, would be a terrific catch, and he didn't have a girlfriend at that time.

Or so I thought! Only later did I find out that the girl who was coming to the wedding with him, who I thought was just a high school friend with whom he had reconnected, was in fact a girlfriend!

The Rehearsal Dinner.
November 1. 7:00 p.m.

All the stress of the day immediately melted away at the Rehearsal Dinner. It was so exciting to see all of our friends and family in the same place—celebrating us! As soon as we arrived, my parents proposed a toast and proceeded to play the most hysterical and touching slide show of Gary's and my lives. I watched in stunned silence wondering how on earth my parents had managed to pull this off along with everything else they were doing. It brought tears to my eyes.

I took a quick opportunity to step back and observe at the Rehearsal Dinner. After this weekend, I realized I'd probably never have all these people assembled together again in my life. Everyone looked so happy, and I suddenly realized it was because of us. Seeing that makes all the stress and planning so worthwhile—-knowing that you are loved by so many people who want nothing more than your happiness.

THE DAY OF DAYS
November 2

The big day has arrived. Morning.

I woke at 7 a.m. and rushed to the window. Peering out, I thought I saw...the sun! Could it be? Unconvinced, I threw open the window and stuck my hand out. Nothing but a brisk cold breeze. I did a silent cheer while lamenting the bride in Boston now dealing with the Perfect Storm that miraculously seems to have passed us by.

It was time to wake everyone in the suite with the great news. Although they didn't seem quite as overjoyed as I was, I prodded them until they got dressed, and we went down to a leisurely breakfast. This was going to be such a great day.

My euphoria quickly disappeared when I returned to the hotel room and saw 150 unfolded programs on the floor. Shoot—I'd forgotten about them! I wonder if I can fold while having my make-up done? Thankfully one of my friends appeared and was given the honor of performing this duty as I ran to my hair and make-up appointments with my bridesmaids.

It was a little unnerving to be the center of attention. I'm far more comfortable celebrating others than being celebrated. I tried to relax and enjoy it, because it will never happen like this again.

The big day has arrived. Morning.

We had a quick breakfast while exchanging greetings with many of our guests in the hotel dining room—a nice relaxed beginning to the day. The weather was cold with a bit of sun, but no rain. That's acceptable.

The next order of business was to obtain an ironing board and iron from housekeeping. That morning the Bride had informed me that her crinoline needed to be "touched up." She neglected to mention until she showed it to me that the bridal salon had warned her that it was a multi-hour task, to be undertaken over several days. What a relief that the Bride had not allowed me to commit to alter the Maid of Honor's dress; I would never have gotten it done!

The Bride and her attendants all had make-up appointments this morning. I had opted to do my own make-up, so I was free to iron and pack all the items that the FOB and BOB would be transporting directly to the wedding site. This included the Bride's bridal gown and all her accoutrements (the list was endless), and mine as well. What an exercise in logistics!

Hair dramas. 12:30 p.m.

I was due to meet the Bride at her hairdresser's salon uptown at 1:00. I had left the hotel room when I got a call from the Bride: The hairstylist needed her bridal headpiece so he could work the hairstyle around it. I went back and located it among the things that were packed to go to the wedding site and took off again.

Traffic was horrendous, and the taxi driver had trouble finding the address. Worst of all, I noticed some spots of rain on the windshield, but decided I would not mention it to the Bride; after all, it might clear up before the time for the pictures.

When I arrived, the Bride was already in the chair and the hair stylist was working on an elaborate "updo." It really looked lovely when he finished. She's gorgeous! He gave my hair a quick wash and style (he couldn't perform a miracle, but he made me look very good indeed!) and we were off in search of a taxi again.

The mad dash. 2:15-3:00 p.m.

I had never seen traffic like it. Forty-five minutes to get from the Upper West Side to SoHo? Was the Polish War Veterans parade this weekend? I thought it was last Saturday.

True to form, we arrived one half-hour later than planned to the Puck Building. With a shock, I realized that this was the exact time Gary had planned to arrive (unlike me, he is very punctual), which meant he might spot me before the photographer's carefully arranged "First Sighting" in fifteen minutes. What a huge catastrophe that would be.

I ducked down low in the taxi and instructed my mother to act as scout. As I tried in vain to keep my five-inch bouffant safely out of sight, I started to feel a little...woozy. With a pang I remembered that since I had gotten everyone up at the crack of dawn to eat breakfast, it had been over seven hours since I ate. Uh-oh.

At this point my mother, being the sensible one, had simply called Gary on his cell and ascertained that he was, in fact, right across the street and getting out of his taxi. Desperate for food and a stall tactic, I did what any sensible bride would: I asked him to get me a slice of pizza.

Arrival at the site. 3:00 p.m.

Pizza? Is she crazy? Images of tomato sauce on a white gown filled my head. Fortunately, the Groom realized the insanity of this request and offered to buy a turkey sub instead. Good thinking—this also might keep him out of the way until we got into the building. She ran into the wedding site, holding a scarf over her face and newly done hair, hiding herself from the Groom in case he was within view. Of course I ran along with her, but couldn't help wondering if it was necessary, as they were going to see each other for pictures before the ceremony anyway. However, mine is not to reason why…

There was no time to lose. The photographer was already there, and we were way behind schedule. We quickly zipped up the gown and he snapped some pictures.

When the Groom arrived with the food, I went out to get it from him, preserving the "no visual contact" rule.

He looked extremely handsome in his tux! The Bride leaned over and we negotiated a few bites of sub to her mouth without dripping anything on the dress. So far, so good.

The photographer then orchestrated the entry of the Bride into the wedding site itself where the Groom was waiting, and memorialized the Groom's first view of her in her wedding attire. Romantic! After a few photographs at the wedding site, the Bride and Groom left with the photographer to take some pictures outside.

The first pictures. 3:30 p.m.

Nothing is more spectacular than seeing your husband-to-be for the first time on your wedding day.

Whether it happens at the altar or a little earlier, nothing compares to the jolt of amazement at seeing the man of your dreams all dressed up to get married to you.

Gary and I had decided to meet before the ceremony to take pictures. We posed outside in SoHo (the sun had disappeared and the clouds were gathering, but no rain would alter my perfect, frizz-free updo) and then took off to Brooklyn to take pictures with the Manhattan skyline behind us.

Funny—people claim it was about 25 degrees that day, with a fierce wind, but I pranced about in my strapless gown for an hour and barely remember feeling cold.

We were so excited that nothing else mattered.

Last-minute preparations and problems.
3:30 p.m.

I now just had time to get into my dress, apply a little makeup and hook on some jewelry before the arrival of the caterer and the florist. The catering staff arrived as scheduled and they began to work on setup.

Everything *seemed* to be on track.

However, the florist had not yet arrived, and it was now one half hour after his scheduled arrival. I heaved a sigh of relief when two deliverymen finally arrived with the floral arrangements. They then placed them on the floor at the entry to the wedding site and promptly turned to leave.

I raced after them and asked when Juan was coming. The deliverymen knew nothing about it! The Bride had paid an extra sum of money for him to come *personally* and supervise the placement of the arrangements and the decorating of the wedding cake with petals, but he was nowhere in sight!

I was distraught. I called the florist shop and was told that Juan was with another delivery, and that the deliverymen knew what to do. A short conversation with them indicated otherwise. I called the florist again. Juan finally came to the phone. Needless to say, we had quite an exchange, which ended with him speaking to the deliveryman on my phone and giving him instructions.

141

The final result was fine. There was not really a great amount of arranging necessary, but I was outraged that the Bride had paid extra for this service, and Juan did not follow through. It offended my sense of fairness.

Was I overreacting? Probably—but I definitely did not need this added stress just a few hours before the wedding.

Furious as I was with the florist, I must say that he had done a beautiful job on the candelabras and the lattice board. I was about to begin to affix the table cards to the ivy, when a few bridesmaids came up to ask if they could help. Absolutely—with gratitude!

The entire bridal party had been asked to be present at 4:00 for photographs. Wonder of wonders, all 17 of them, plus the Bride and Groom and four parents, were there on time. The photographer was a dream. Always a smile on his face and a personality and patter that made you smile, too. He was worth whatever we paid for him. He must have taken several hundred photographs, every possible combination of bridal party and family.

The videographer was fine too, but when he catches you unaware and asks you for a comment, it's a bit difficult to focus on what you're saying when you're trying to think of a million other details. I have no idea at all what I said. I wish I had thought to prepare some comments in advance.

In a trance. 4:30 p.m.

When we arrived back at the wedding site, there was a flurry of excitement. All the bridesmaids and groomsmen had arrived, the caterers were setting up the ceremony area, and my poor mother was darting about looking frantic.

"Juan sent a deliveryman to set up the flowers and decorate the cake, and he has no idea what's going on! I just called Juan and yelled at him in Spanish!"

I smiled serenely at my mother. "That's nice. Gary and I had a great time taking pictures."

"Did you see the flowers he used for the head table? He used regular lilies instead of callas—it's not what we asked for! And the color is all wrong! I yelled at him about that too..."

I waved my bouquet in front of her. "Speaking of callas, did you see how beautiful this is?"

My mother looked like she didn't recognize me. Who had kidnapped her daughter? I wandered off to talk to my bridesmaids.

The rehearsal—A formula for disaster. 5:30 p.m.

With the floral predicament resolved, I started to think ahead about the next challenge. I'd been worried about the ceremony from the moment I had learned the Rehearsal Dinner would not, in fact, include a rehearsal. (How presumptuous of me to assume this!) Since the priest and rabbi were coming in from out of town for the wedding day only, the Bride had informed me that we'd "just practice a couple of hours before the actual ceremony." She kept telling me to relax, and assured me that this would be no problem. The FOB went even further and suggested it would be better as all the instructions would be fresh in our minds.

I quickly learned that was not the case. First, it was utterly *impossible* to get everyone together. Some of the groomsmen were milling about, others were chatting among themselves; still others were on cell phones. It was a mess! (The bridesmaids, naturally, being women and eager to do things right, were exactly where they should have been.)

I then found out the Bride and Groom had not discussed anything with the priest and rabbi about the ceremony—preferring to "wing it." Am I old-fashioned in thinking that weddings are not to be winged?

This was to be a traditional ceremony in no sense of the word! First, the Bride disagreed with the rabbi about the processional. She may have given up being married in a church, but she had always envisioned going down the aisle on the arm of her father, and that was how it was going to be. It was decided that our son would escort me, FOB would escort the Bride, and the

Groom would be escorted by both his parents in the traditional Jewish way.

The rabbi also thought the ushers should escort the bridesmaids down the aisle, but it was decided that the ushers would stand up front, awaiting the procession of the Bride, as in a Christian ceremony. Let me mention that the rabbi had tremendous patience with this unusual situation.

The rest of it was just as mix-and-match. After escorting me, the BOB would return to the back to escort the grandmother of the Bride as a part of the processional, but the grandmother of the Groom was unsure of her ability to walk down the aisle, so she would be seated before the processional. And, since we had a different number of bridesmaids and ushers, some of the groomsmen would have to escort two bridesmaids during the recessional. Would anyone recognize this as a wedding?

As if to emphasize the non-traditional, the recessional music chosen by the Bride and Groom was "The Irish Washerwoman." This appeared just a touch surreal for my daughter, the self-proclaimed feminist!

At this point, forget tradition—I just wanted the ceremony to go off without a major disaster.

The rehearsal. 5:45 p.m.

Why is everyone spazzing out? It's just a rehearsal. Who cares who goes where—it doesn't matter as long as no one trips. Besides, everyone will be focused on me, as it should be.

My mother and some bridesmaids felt differently. They were clamoring for order, but it was impossible to hear anything above the din of the groomsmen and Gary's six nieces and nephews running around yelling.

In a dreamlike state, I looked at Gary. He is so handsome—how did I ever get so lucky? And he's so chill—just hanging out, completely unfazed by all the racket. That's just one of the many qualities I love about him: He's the ultimate unflappable Type B personality. So opposite of me—that's why we're perfect together! Except I'm feeling strangely Type B myself right now. Nothing's going to intrude on this exquisite feeling of complete and total rightness.

The main event—The ceremony. 6:30 p.m.

It's all a blur! Somehow, BOB escorted me down the aisle, placed me correctly at the back of the altar, facing the guests, and the FOB escorted the Bride, managed to turn back her veil without dislodging it, kissed her, and then joined me. I know the seven bridesmaids were all to my left, looking beautiful, with a number of them crying. I can picture the Maid of Honor, who had thought to bring a tissue in case of tears, standing to the side of the Bride. I remember the four Groomsmen and two Best Men (or at least one of them) joking and laughing in response to the comments of the FOG. I recall that the battery-powered lighters I had brought to ensure that we could light the candles were a disaster. No one could operate them, and the priest asked why we didn't have matches! But that too was another occasion for laughter. Nothing was going to spoil this event.

My clearest memory is the joy and love so evident on the faces of the Bride and Groom as the ceremony was conducted. I think the Jewish tradition of having the parents at the altar is wonderful! The fact that FOB and I were able to stand just a few feet away from the Bride and Groom, facing them, and watch them make their vows is something never to be forgotten.

I'm glad I remembered that much because a few minutes later, a combination of the fact that I had not had anything to eat or drink since breakfast, had been continuously on edge, and was wearing a heavy, hot, beaded dress, took its toll. I fought the feeling for a while, then clutched FOB's hand and told him he'd better hold me up or I was going to faint. He rose to the occasion and kept me in an upright position.

It got worse rather than better. I had to either sit down, or I would fall down. What could I do with the least people, and most especially not the Bride, noticing me? As luck would have it, there was a rather wide windowsill about two feet in back of me. I waited for a point in the ceremony when the Bride and Groom were handing roses to the POG. I backed up to the windowsill and leaned against it. Wonderful cool air reached me through the window—yes, that was better. Uh-oh, the Bride and Groom were about to turn around. I bolted upright. One more quick lean against the window when no one was looking, and I knew I was going to make it!

The main event—The ceremony.
6:30 p.m.

A few minutes before the ceremony I suddenly realized that I was about to get married—in front of 175 people! It was a thought that made me clench my father's arm in a death grip. He looked at me and raised an eyebrow slightly: "You ready for this Sheila?" he teased. How grateful I am that he's so eternally relaxed and unruffled. At that moment, I realize it's the same quality that has drawn me to Gary—that ability to exert a calming effect no matter how chaotic the situation. (Which, around my mother and me recently, is a great deal of the time.)

The music started playing and, before I knew it, I was down at the altar with Gary. The ceremony was a wonderful blur—I remember that I was crying and my nose wouldn't stop running—and walking up the aisle afterward was the most exhilarating feeling. I'm

*married to the most amazing guy in the world! Gary
and I slipped away to spend a few moments celebrating
us before we hit the cocktail hour.*

The main event—The cocktail hour.
7:00 p.m.

The cocktail reception went beautifully. The Bride and
Groom had chosen not to have a formal receiving line
after the wedding, but rather to greet their guests
informally during the cocktail reception. This was a
nice alternative since it permitted freedom of
movement for all involved and avoided the long waits
associated with receiving lines. On the other hand, it
meant that not all members of the bridal party would
meet all guests—a tradeoff, but a worthwhile one, I
think.

The sushi station, which I had greatly maligned due to
the additional cost, was a big hit! And the hors
d'oeuvres were fantastic. There was a buzz of
conversation and everyone seemed to be enjoying
themselves. Was it time to relax yet?

At the end of the cocktail hour, guests were
encouraged to move into the reception area, and the
band started to play. Still on course. Then I heard the
MOG saying that she and the FOG had nowhere to sit.
How could that be? I checked out the head table, where
we had decided that the Bride and Groom, POB and
POG would be seated together. A tiny table had been
set for two people! Apparently the catering captain had

149

not been able to find the head table plan, so he had assumed it was just for the Bride and Groom. Staff quickly broke down the tiny table, located a larger one and set it for the six of us. Okay, another emergency dealt with.

The main event—The Cocktail Hour. 7:00 p.m.

The cocktail hour was great. It was so exciting to see all our favorite people! As we circulated, friends kept bringing us plates of sushi and hors d'oeuvres. Gary and I must have become the first couple to taste absolutely every morsel of food at their wedding! Looking around, I realized my bridesmaids were voluntarily wearing their wraps. And they looked great with the black dresses. Maybe Mom knows something about wedding fashion, after all.

When the guests were asked to enter the dining area, I saw them effortlessly plucking their name cards off the ivy-covered lattice board. What a relief! And it looked fabulous, too—my mother is so creative! I could never have pulled that off.

Just before Gary and I were announced and entered the dining area, I saw my mother speaking to the head captain and looking worried. Apparently the caterers set up the wrong-sized head table. By the time we entered the reception, however, it was all cleared up.

After our (unofficial) first dance, Gary and I started to make the rounds. I admired the votives the caterers had artfully arranged on each table—the fishbowl shape my mother picked out looked fantastic! Admittedly, before I saw them, I wasn't sure, but they exceeded even my precise wedding quality standards. And the candlelight effect perfectly masked the not-quite-burgundy hue my color-blind friend Juan had chosen for a few arrangements.

I sighed contentedly. This would be a perfect night.

The main event—The reception. 8:00 p.m.

After a few songs, the band asked the dancers to be seated and four of us moved to the front. FOB and I welcomed the guests, and thanked the POG for their many contributions. I explained the *Coupe de Mariage*, from which the newly wedded couple would drink their first toast. FOB then proposed the first toast to the Bride and Groom, and the godfathers of the Bride and Groom offered grace.

Good, I thought, "I can heave a sigh of relief and begin to enjoy myself." A salad course was served—excellent again. I was beginning to think I could stop worrying about the food too. Okay, were we on course with the program? Wait, did the band forget to introduce the bridal party? Oh well, there are worse things that could happen.

The main event—The reception.
8:00 p.m.

Before I knew it, we were being toasted and applauded. Then the caterers served us a selection of each of the entrees we had so carefully chosen, and they were fabulous! Well worth our time and effort.

Suddenly, I heard Rozz announcing the dance to "our song," and Gary led me onto the dance floor.

Rozz has one of the most amazing voices I've ever heard. We saw her sing at one of our favorite lounges a few months before the wedding, and I was so thrilled Gary had chosen her. Given that her voice is perfectly suited to Aretha Franklin covers, Gary and I ultimately decided on "You're All I Need to Get By" for our song—an Aretha hit that perfectly summed it up. Gary emailed Rozz with a list of all the songs we wanted for our dance, and the dances with our parents, and Rozz said no problem.

That's why I found it so strange to hear the notes of "My Wild Irish Rose" start to play. Gary and I sashayed to the front of the room.

"This isn't our song—this is the song Sheila and her father are dancing to!" Gary hissed to Rozz.

Rozz had a look of shock and dismay on her face. The band abruptly stopped playing and she huddled with them. Gary and I waited, both of us with that sinking

152

feeling: Maybe Rozz doesn't know our song? Nah, couldn't be.

The look on her face when she returned said it all.

She's sorry, somehow the multiple emails and phone conversations between her and Gary about the songs we wanted weren't sufficient, and her band doesn't know our song. But she can play another Aretha song instead!

We didn't want another Aretha song—we wanted that one. If we had been a bit more quick-thinking, we could have popped in the Aretha Franklin CD that was packed up with the wedding CD's. But we were in such a state of shock, we told her to pick a love-themed Aretha tune and get on with it. Which she did.

As we whirled around the room, I put it in perspective: everyone I know has had things go wrong at the reception. Plus, I would gladly trade this for the good weather we got. So many worse things could have happened—this was no big deal. Besides, bad things happen in threes, right? Which, counting the wrong-sized head table, Rozz playing the wrong song, and then her not knowing the right song, makes three.

Right?

More to come. 9:00 p.m.

Between the salad and the entrée, we were beginning to make our rounds to converse with our guests. As I was speaking with some relatives, I noticed that my aunt, with whom I have always been very close, didn't seem well. Her health is not good, but she loves the Bride so dearly that she was determined to make it to the wedding to see her married. As I watched in horror, she practically fainted in her chair.

I called to the catering staff, and they carried her to the back, away from the noise and commotion. We called 911, as I prayed. Her husband, children, FOB and I could only wait anxiously with her until the ambulance crew arrived.

More to come. 9:45 p.m..

Following our first dance, lots of people joined us on the dance floor. After a few songs, I noticed my parents were nowhere to be found. Must be off talking with guests somewhere. After a few more songs, they still hadn't materialized. Even stranger, Gary seemed quite intent on keeping me on the dance floor. Suddenly I panicked: Had something happened to my parents? I dragged Gary in search of them.

We found my brother at the bar area, where he began anxiously making small talk with me while simultaneously blocking the entrance to the bridal suite hallway. Now I knew something was wrong. I pushed past him and saw my father standing in the hallway. At least he was all right. "What's wrong.

Where's Mom?" I was completely panicked at this point, and there was a roar in my ears. I heard my father saying gently that my aunt had passed away.

I slumped against the wall. My knees were weak. I couldn't believe this was happening! My aunt was dead? We needed to stop this reception.

I moved closer to the wall of EMT workers. Glancing over them, I saw my aunt sitting in a chair with an oxygen mask, looking at me with tired eyes. "I'm so confused—what's going on?" I asked my father.

"Like I told you, she passed out, but she's come to. She seems fine, but they're going to take her to the hospital, just in case."

What a relief that I had heard him wrong at first! I was so happy I started crying. Unfortunately, the emotional roller coaster of the past hour had taken its toll on me, and I suddenly couldn't stand anymore. Gary and I sat down and requested some much-needed wine.

The crisis subsides. 11:30 p.m..

After taking her vital signs and giving her some oxygen, the ambulance crew said that my aunt seemed all right. The outcome? I learned that she was on a new medication and was feeling amazingly well—so well that, although she never drinks, she had a glass of champagne to celebrate. The combination of the new medication and champagne must have caused the dizziness.

Despite their reassurances, I was still sick with worry and in somewhat of a daze. I'm a little confused about what happened when, but I remember the Bride and FOB having their dance to "My Wild Irish Rose."

They were such a vision together that it brought me back a bit.

I also remember the Bride and Groom dancing together. They looked so happy! Before my eyes, my daughter was having her dream wedding. I reflected on how lucky they were to have found each other. I know from firsthand experience what a wonderful person our daughter is, and Gary seems to be the perfect match for her.

Suddenly, I remembered my wedding coordinator role! I realized that the scheduled time for the Best Men's toasts had come and gone without a peep from either of them. I tracked down Rozz, who was eating in the back, and asked if she would announce the toasts. She was very agreeable, but I couldn't help wondering if she had even looked at the schedule we had provided.

The Bride and Groom and most of the guests were out on the dance floor for the band's entire last set. Looking at them dancing and enjoying themselves, I breathed another sigh of relief. We had done it!

The aftermath.
November 3. 12:30 a.m.

It was a success and it was over! I looked around the room—what a mess. The caterers were busy putting things away and cleaning up. During the last hour or so, I had heard quite a number of dishes crashing.

Possibly they had decided it would be easier to break them than to pack them back up?

Luckily, we had arranged to have a locked closet to store items until the next day, so we did not have to parade through the streets of NYC carrying candelabra. And I had to make sure the caterers didn't leave with our precious silver overlays. They joined the other items already in the closet. However, the pile of things we had to take with us quickly mounted: the street clothes we had arrived in, train, veil, assorted baskets, and more. Where did we get all this stuff? And more importantly, how were we going to get it all into a taxi?

•

The aftermath.
November 3, 12:30 a.m.

Suddenly the lights were on and people were kissing us goodbye! Wait—it's already over?

With the blur of all the last-minute honeymoon planning, we realized Gary had forgotten to book transportation from the wedding to our hotel. Which wouldn't have been a big deal except that we were now married to six large candelabra, too. The Puck Building staff stashed them in a closet, and we headed outside to hail a cab. Climbing into a taxi in a wedding dress will make for a New York moment.

Except that we couldn't seem to hail a cab. Even more distressing, we noticed several other family members trying to hail taxis as well. Ten minutes passed with no cab in sight. I was starting to wonder if we'd be there all night.

Just then, like out of a dream, a white stretch limousine pulled up in front of us, and the driver stuck his head out: "$200 and I'll take ya anywhere in the city!"

Our last reunion.
November 3. 1:00 a.m.

I didn't know where the POG, the BOB, or the Bride and Groom had gone. FOB and I went out to the street loaded down with our allotted items, and began to look for one of the taxis, which we had been assured were always plentiful at this wedding site. Not one in sight. At least, not an unoccupied one.

As we unsuccessfully tried to hail taxis, we heard someone shouting at us and turned around. There were the Bride and Groom, who had hailed a passing limo, and they were yelling at us to get in. This was great timing! We got in, traveled about 30 feet, and almost ran over the BOB and POG trying to hail a cab as well.

How did everyone get taxis except the wedding party? We rolled up to them and they hopped in, too.

What an end to the evening! The limo was like a traveling bordello, replete with soft lights, music and heart designs. We dropped the BOB off first, and as the POG, FOB and I alighted at our hotel, we saw the unforgettable vision of our newly married children sailing off into the night in the white limousine.

ONE MORE DAY OF CELEBRATION
November 3

The day after. 9:30 a.m..

Most brides will tell you that the day after their wedding brings a feeling of complete and total relief. Unfortunately, it wasn't that way for me. Although I couldn't be more thrilled that Gary and I were married, I woke up the next day feeling very unsettled. Why? Well, because I knew that my mother didn't have a great time at my wedding. How could she? She was trying to keep track of a million details, her aunt-who's-like-a-mother had to be taken to the emergency room, and then I discovered she had tripped over a suitcase the night before and practically broken her foot. Which is why she wasn't dancing, despite spending countless hours practicing with my father. It struck me as supremely unfair that the woman who had devoted the past six months to making sure I had the wedding of my dreams had so many bad things happen at it.

And it's my fault. The Great Wedding Spirit was clearly sending me a message. That I deserved it! I was too demanding, too selfish, too emotional about everything during the planning process. She probably tripped on the suitcase because she was so exhausted from making all those overlays.

So at 9:00 a.m. I slipped out of bed and called her on my cell phone. Before she could say anything, I broke down crying and told her how sorry I was that the wedding was so disastrous for her. Of course, she didn't understand what I was saying, and seemed to think that I hadn't enjoyed my wedding. Well, I was enjoying it until I realized that she wasn't having a good time. The irony of it all wasn't lost on me, but I couldn't help myself. She reassured me over and over again that she had a wonderful time, simply because she had been able to see me get married. Which I regarded with some skepticism, because it sounds like one of those things mothers have to say to their daughters.

After 15 minutes of sobbing in the Westin lobby, I finally pulled myself together and Gary and I left for the brunch. Food always helps.

The day after. 9:30 a.m.

I checked on my aunt's status first thing and learned that after she had gotten some oxygen and some sleep, she had signed herself out of the hospital early that morning. That was a wonderful start to my day.

Then I got a call from the Bride. We talked a bit about the wedding, debriefing it. She sounded so depressed, and I couldn't figure out where this was coming from.

Hadn't she just had a wonderful wedding? Wasn't she married to a man she loved? Is there such a thing as a post-wedding depression?

Well, apparently the problems stemmed from me. Somehow, she had the feeling that I hadn't enjoyed myself, and she was feeling terrible about it. But I did have a wonderful time! I kept trying to convince the Bride that her wedding had been everything I had hoped for, but I didn't seem to be getting through to her.

Maybe I had created some of her depression by not saying the right thing when we first began to talk. I thought back. I had mentioned a few things that went wrong and we had discussed them. But I had expected things to go wrong—they always do when you have a big event—and there was nothing catastrophic. By the time we hung up, she sounded a little better.

The hotel lobby this morning was full of wedding guests. Everyone had very complimentary things to say about the wedding and their NYC weekend in general. That sent my spirits soaring again.

The post-wedding brunch was held in one of those little Irish taverns that are so prevalent in NYC. The food was terrific, and it was such fun seeing everyone one more time, especially now that the stress was over.

The Bride and Groom came in a bit later than the 11:00 starting time and joined most of the younger crowd upstairs.

After brunch we had one last wedding chore to complete before heading home. A number of the newlyweds' possessions had ended up in our hotel suite and needed to be transported to their apartment.

Upon arriving, we found the Bride and Groom and a group of the wedding party watching television in a half-comatose state. The non-stop festivities of the weekend had taken their toll.

We were feeling it too, and were more than ready to start our long drive back to CP, satisfied and happy with the wedding weekend. And another bonus—when we reached home, we would once again have our dining room, laundry room and basement area released from their wedding captivity and restored to their normal uses.

AFTERWORD
November 6 to 25

The honeymoon—Day 3.
November 6.

I've started here because I honestly don't remember anything from the first two days. Gary and I slept, lay on the beach, slept some more and drank lots of frozen concoctions with little umbrellas in them. It was heaven.

Finally, we roused ourselves to more athletic pursuits, and headed to the tennis courts.

Except that I was having some difficulty concentrating. Now that I was out of my post-wedding coma, I had started replaying details of the wedding in my mind.

169

Denise A. Kelly and Sheila Kelly Kaplan

It hit me in the middle of my serve toss in the second set: "Oh my God!" I screamed, and crumpled into a heap on the court.

Gary ran over, looking aghast and like he was trying to remember CPR. "What's wrong? What is it?"

"I thought my cousins Judy and Jerry were your cousins Geri and Jerry!" I wailed.

"So? Who cares?"

"So they came up to me to say hello, and I was introducing them as your cousins and then I asked them about the costume party your great-uncle had— remember, the one for his birthday? No wonder they looked at me like I was crazy. And then I got pulled away by someone else, and never realized what I did. I can't believe I did that!"

"They probably didn't even notice."

"Oh, yes they did. And I am such a complete idiot for not remembering them. She looks exactly the same as she did when I was in fifth grade—the last time I saw them."

"You haven't seen them since fifth grade? Why on earth should you remember them after all these years?"

"I have to call them right now and apologize."

"Honey, if that's what you want to do, I totally support you, but honestly, we're in Barbados and I don't think it's that big a deal. If you want, you can give them a call when we get back. But I wouldn't worry about it— I'm sure they've totally forgotten by now."

He had started to work his magic. "Really, you think so? I mean, I know who they are, it's just that Geri and Judy look exactly alike, and with all those 'Jerrys' around, I just got totally confused."

"Of course, sweetie. It's not your fault. Besides, I'm sure it happens all the time at weddings. Come on, let's get you a frozen drink."

Sun-baked thoughts. November 14.

There's nothing like lying in the sun for 14 days straight to experience some serious epiphanies. Which I'm now going to share with you:

Epiphany #1: Paybacks will be hell. During my tumultuous adolescence, I remember thinking that I would probably be "blessed" with a daughter who is ten times more difficult than I was with my mother, because I had brought it on myself with my bad behavior. Current assessment? I'll probably have all daughters, and once the horror of adolescence wears off, they will all get engaged the same year, with wedding dates only days apart. I will be tasked with sewing all the linens, performing calligraphy on the

171

invites, menus and programs, and perhaps even mixing drinks at the reception. All of which I will do with a smile on my face, because it is my karmic destiny.

Epiphany #2: Epiphany #1 notwithstanding, it was all worth it. All the craziness, foibles and mishaps conspired to make a wedding that was breathtakingly beautiful, and resoundingly human. It also created endless entertaining stories for all the other newlyweds we met on the honeymoon. And most importantly, it allowed me to marry, in just six short months, the man of my dreams, my soul mate and my best friend.

Epiphany #3: I shouldn't have freaked out so much about everything.

In retrospect. November 14.

Re: She's married!
A few days after we got home, I was looking out the kitchen window one day and suddenly thought: Our daughter is married, and we have this terrific new son-in-law. I think I must have been so focused on all the preparations and details that it took several days for me to process the thought that they are actually married.

Re: The florist
We got an incredible amount of value for our money. The flowers were beautiful, although one third of the table centerpieces did not contain the flowers or exact colors we had agreed upon. If we had known

beforehand the hassle we would have with the florist sending deliverymen rather than coming himself, we probably would still have gone with that florist just for the huge savings.

Re: The rehearsal
I'm still stunned by the disorganization of the rehearsal. Perhaps the bridal party had been in so many ceremonies that they didn't need the rehearsal. I know that I certainly did. I'm still not sure how the recessional went since I "recessed" before most of the others. It wasn't until I saw pictures a few weeks after the wedding that I realized that the grandmother of the Bride was escorted out on the arms of the Catholic priest and the Jewish rabbi. I'm sure she loved it!

Re: The band
The music was excellent. It's a shame that the high quality of the music was offset by the band's failure to follow through with what was expected of them. We provided a very-detailed schedule and instructions for them, and they assured the Bride and Groom that they knew all the songs they had requested. I'm still at a loss as to what we could have done differently to avoid the problems we had.

Re: The organization
There shouldn't have been so many things left until the last minute. And the Bride was right—we should have hired a coordinator for the wedding day to keep things on track. Unless someone else handles all the details, answers the caterer's questions, solves problems as

they come up, finds missing items, and reminds people of what should be going on next, the MOB will feel as though she's the circus-master and needs to oversee everything. And I did. Live and learn…except that she's my one and only daughter, so I won't be organizing any more weddings.

Re: Dealing with the Bride
I wish I had found some way to help alleviate the Bride's stress. I should have been more prepared for her to break into hysterical tears at least once the day before the wedding, and the day after too. If I had it to do over again, I would not have let her know that anything about her wedding was less than perfect or a hassle in any way. And…somehow, I should have known to ask the Bride in advance if her crinoline needed to be ironed.

Re: Being the MOB
Despite the problems and missteps, I had a wonderful time at the wedding. The joy of seeing our daughter married to the man she loves was overwhelming! How could anything surpass that?

Post-honeymoon bliss. November 21.

We had two presents waiting for us when we returned from the honeymoon: our wedding video and six candelabra covered with dead flowers. Right, I forgot—I own them. I spent about four hours picking all the wilted blooms off, then vainly tried to stuff the candelabra into the hall closet. They didn't fit. In our 800-square foot apartment, there's nowhere else for them to go. Why is Mom always right? We finally got creative and used four of them as speaker holders in the living room.

The wedding video was another treat. After watching it one time through, we fast-forwarded to our favorite part: when we started dancing and realized Rozz was playing the wrong song. It's hilarious, and we take to playing it for all our friends in slow-motion frame-advance to see every horrific facial expression in greater detail. Wow, that was money well spent!

Regular married life. November 22.

It's so great I have to gush a little. Remember when you were little and dreamed about finding the perfect man? And then when you actually started dating, and the great disillusionment settled in? All those lukewarm dates, all those phone calls to your mother and friends lamenting your seemingly eternal single status.

It can be quite a shock to realize that the energy spent asserting your independence and scorning people who can't function without a relationship can now be channeled into a marriage. With a guy you can call 15 times a day without appearing too forward, go faucet-shopping with, and reveal your secret love of Scrabble to.

Yes, get ready: You are about to become the person you and your single friends once mocked. And you're going to love it.

Withdrawal pains. November 22.

I feel bereft! Of course I'm delighted that our daughter and her husband are so happy, but I miss talking to her. We communicated so much during all those months of wedding planning that it's twice as hard not to have it now. But I'm determined that Gary will not ever think of me as an interfering mother-in-law. They have their own lives to lead now, and I know how busy they are. So I'm going to restrain myself from calling just to chat. I know they'll call when they have time, and of course, I'll break down and call them whenever I can think of a good excuse.

Being a daughter and a wife. November 25.

Shortly after we returned from our honeymoon, I realized my mother was avoiding me. I wouldn't be shocked if she needed a break from all the drama, but it did seem a little strange. On several occasions, over a week would pass without her calling, which was highly unusual. When I finally asked if anything was wrong, she hesitated and then confessed her fear that she would seem too intrusive if she called too often.

Apparently, now that I was married, things were different.

I was shocked. How can calling once or twice a week be considered overly intrusive? When I thought about it from her perspective, though, I could see her point: She wanted me to make my "new" family a priority, and didn't want to interfere in that. And I was very grateful for her sensitivity.

Except that I still needed my mom! Just as much as before. We finally agreed that she would call me on Sunday nights, and that if I wanted to talk more often, I should call her. Of course, the near-daily emailing would continue.

The funny thing is: Things will change. Not in the ways you expect, though. It's not a dramatic change, but over time, as you make all your major decisions with another person, inevitably this will include decisions about your respective families. You'll no longer be free to say you'll fly to California next Christmas with the rest of the family without discussing it with your husband first.

The good part is that it will also bring you closer to your mother in ways you didn't expect. Suddenly, you can spend hours discussing your new window treatments, and she can (finally!) share her infinite wisdom on salmon preparation.

You will also start to feel like part of a legacy—a connection to both your past and to the generation that you may create. The significance of these family ties will cause you to perform remarkably selfless acts, like volunteering to spend Fourth of July vacation with your adorable-but-exhausting nieces and nephews because you want your husband to be their favorite uncle.

In other words, you'll see yourself starting to act surprisingly like...well, your mother. Except the comparison may feel strangely flattering. You can never repay your mom for all she's done. But maybe that's the best way to start.

ONE LAST WORD

from the MOB:

Despite what my daughter insists, there was never any such band as "The Crab Cakes." In her pre-nuptial anxiety, she seems to have developed amnesia. The band was actually called "BT and the Cruisers" and they were terrific! I'll bet they would have known "You're All I Need to Get By" by Aretha Franklin, too!

from the Bride:

Does anyone need to borrow any candelabra?

...and they lived
happily ever after.

THE END

About the Authors

This mother/daughter writing team was a natural outcome of the mother/daughter wedding planning team which functioned the previous year. Denise Kelly, mother, lives and writes in Central Pennsylvania, while daughter Sheila Kelly Kaplan, lives, works and writes in Manhattan, NY.

Printed in the United States
15591LVS00001B/22

9 781410 795533